Spreading God's Word By Telling Your Story

GOD CAN USE YOU TOO!

Gaynor van der Hagen

SOLOMON
KEY PUBLISHING

LONDON, UNITED KINGDOM

Copyright © 2024 by Gaynor van der Hagen.

All rights reserved. No part of this publication may be reproduced, distributed or transmitted in any form or by any means, including photocopying, recording, or other electronic or mechanical methods, without the prior written permission of the publisher, except in the case of brief quotations embodied in critical reviews and certain other non-commercial uses permitted by copyright law.

Gaynor van der Hagen / Solomon Key Publishing

Photography: Meryl Yates

Spreading God's Word By Telling Your Story / Gaynor van der Hagen. —First ed.

ISBN: 9798321579503

I dedicate this book to my loving and faithful husband, Paul, and our wonderful children, Samuel, Deborah, Rebecca, and Joshua. I am so blessed to have such a supportive family who encourages me to fulfil my dreams.

I invite you to join me as I share how I came to know Jesus as my Lord and Saviour. I trust that my story and the unique opportunities God has given me to share His love with others will inspire and encourage you to do the same. Thank you for taking an interest. May you be abundantly blessed!

Gaynor van der Hagen,
Surrey, UK, April 2024

"You know the saying, 'Four months between planting and harvest.' But I say, wake up and look around. The fields are already ripe for harvest."
John 4:35

CONTENTS

FOREWORD I

PREFACE III

My Story 1

"Is It God Speaking?" "How Can We Recognise His Voice?" 9

Ice Cream Anyone? 13

Helen and an Encounter With the Holy Spirit 17

Our Second Meeting 23

The Unexpected 31

Charlotte 37

Is This the End of the World? 41

Sharing the Gospel Effectively 53

The Stay-At-Home Christian 57

A Chip Off The Old Block 63

"O death, where is your victory?" "O death, where is your sting?" 67

Sharing Our Faith In Jesus 75

Peace In Turmoil 85

"A Cup Of Tea Dad?" "Oh, Yes Please!!!" 89

Take The Plunge 95

Christmas In The Sun 99

Who Would Have Thought?! 103

Don't Miss It! 111

How Can I Pray For The Lost? 117

How Can I Accept Jesus as My Lord and Saviour?
.... 119

EPILOGUE 123

REFERENCES 125

FOREWORD

Monica Collard
Senior Pastor
Equippers Church, Surrey

Gaynor has many strengths, one being her love to champion the people around her. She has story after story of reaching out to others, regardless of where she finds herself. Her passion to share Jesus with others is inspiring, and you will enjoy and appreciate her honesty from the real-life experiences she so vulnerably shares.

With her huge heart to encourage and love others, Gaynor is a gatherer of people. She sees those that others might overlook and has a wonderful way of connecting and speaking life to them.

In this book, Gaynor writes in such a way that you will want to look for more opportunities to share your story!

PREFACE

*"Arise, Jerusalem! Let your
light shine for all to see.
For the glory of the Lord
rises to shine on you."*
Isaiah 60:1

IN THIS BOOK, I recount some unique opportunities where the Holy Spirit has enabled me to talk to non-Christians about Jesus, or has led me to encourage Christians at a timely moment. Some people I spoke to were ready to give their lives to Jesus soon after I shared my story, while others have been introduced to Him and are still on a journey. Some are not "yet" interested, but I haven't given up on them. Each time we get to share our faith with someone, it is an opportunity to sow seeds into that person's life, and I believe, and am praying that God will enable these seeds to grow. In Chapter 13, "Sharing Our Faith In Jesus", I have given some suggestions on how to do just that. Of course, each situation is different, and we must be flexible and rely entirely on the Holy Spirit. In

Chapter 20, I have included a prayer acronym to help structure your prayer on how to pray for the lost.

> *"Now listen to the explanation of the parable about the farmer planting seeds: The seed that fell on the footpath represents those who hear the message about the Kingdom and don't understand it. Then the evil one comes and snatches away the seed that was planted in their hearts. The seed on the rocky soil represents those who hear the message and immediately receive it with joy. But since they don't have deep roots, they don't last long. They fall away as soon as they have problems or are persecuted for believing God's word. The seed that fell among the thorns represents those who hear God's word, but all too quickly the message is crowded out by the worries of this life and the lure of wealth, so no fruit is produced. The seed that fell on good soil represents those who truly hear and understand God's word and produce a harvest of thirty, sixty, or even a hundred times as much as had been planted!"* Matthew 13:18-23

Recently, I read the following:

"At a conference some years ago, the speaker before me said, and I quote, "It takes eighteen times for a man to hear the Gospel before he can make a decision". I followed him, thanked him for his remarks, and said that I presume it is the nineteenth whenever I preach, and it's time for a decision.

I love this pastor's faith. He expects the Holy Spirit to move powerfully when he preaches and for those not yet saved to give their lives to Jesus.

However, the above is a good reminder that many individuals need to hear the Gospel several times before they make a decision. Therefore, we must be persistent and never give up on those who seem disinterested.

As Christians, we have an anointing which is primarily to benefit others. *"But you have an anointing from the Holy One, and all of you know the truth."* 1 John 2:20

> *"And it is impossible to please God without faith. Anyone who wants to come to him must believe that God exists and that he rewards those who sincerely seek him."* Hebrews 11:6

The anointing (initiated by faith) enables us to tell others about Jesus. Hebrews 11:6 reminds us that we should spend quality time in His presence. We should prepare our hearts to hear from Him daily by reading His Word and praying, and in so doing, "sincerely seeking Him" and developing a relationship with Him. God loves it when we do this, and He will speak to us and prepare us for whatever He may want to do through us each day.

Friends have said that I have a gift to talk about Jesus to those I don't know well. My response to them is that most of the time, I do it afraid. (There are many reasons why one can feel afraid, which I will explain later in Chapter 13, "Sharing Our Faith In Jesus"). You may then ask me, "Why do you bother to put yourself through all this?" My response is that I love Jesus, and I am so grateful for what He has done for me, knowing that His heart's desire is *"not wanting anyone to perish, but everyone to come to repentance."* (2 Peter 3:9). I have a longing to help bring as many people with me into heaven as I possibly can. God has chosen to work through His people, and I want to be one of them that He uses for His glory:

> *"Work hard so you can present yourself to God and receive his approval. Be a good worker, one who does not need to be ashamed and who correctly explains the word of truth."* 2 Timothy 2:15

Acts 1:4-5, 8 says, *"Do not leave Jerusalem until the Father sends you the gift he promised, as I told you before. John baptized with water, but in just a few days you will be baptized with the Holy Spirit. "But you will receive power when the Holy Spirit comes upon you. And you will be my witnesses, telling people about me everywhere—in Jerusalem, throughout Judea, in Samaria, and to the ends of the earth."*

God gives us power when His Holy Spirit comes upon us to do His will, and we should not try to do anything for Him if we don't have the conviction that He is with us.

"For God wanted them to know that the riches and glory of Christ are for you Gentiles, too. And this is the secret: Christ lives in you. This gives you assurance of sharing his glory." Colossians 1:27

SPREADING GOD'S WORD BY TELLING YOUR STORY

People are hungry for the supernatural (above and beyond the natural) and we need to point them to the "Source" of the supernatural. We are unable to do this unless we are living by His power.

> "Now all glory to God, who is able, through his mighty power at work within us, to accomplish infinitely more than we might ask or think."
> Ephesians 3:20

> "For the Kingdom of God is not just a lot of talk; it is living by God's power." 1 Corinthians 4:20

Be encouraged as you read what God has done, knowing that as you spend time with Him each day and receive His anointing by faith, God will use you too, wherever you may go for His glory; you just need to be willing.

N.B. This book is based on personal experiences, however, for the sake of confidentiality, some of the names of the individuals have been changed.

CHAPTER 1

My Story

"Surely your goodness and unfailing love will pursue me all the days of my life, and I will live in the house of the LORD forever."

Psalm 23:6

I WAS BORN TO Christian parents in Harare, Zimbabwe. My family went to church every Sunday, and we prayed together regularly. I was seven years old when I heard God's audible voice; He simply called my name. I heard Him call me when I was in my parents' garden, and I immediately went to my Grandmother (who lived next door) to ask her if she had called me; it wasn't her. The second time I heard my name called that day, I went to ask my mum if it was her, and she said, "No." Again it happened a third time shortly after that, and neither my Mum nor my Gran knew who it was. We soon forgot about it.

When I was 13, I attended an event at a church in Harare with my youth club; a visiting evangelist from South Africa had been invited to preach. During the meeting, I had an overwhelming sense that God was speaking directly to me through the preacher, and I could feel His immense love for me. It was as if the sermon had been written just for me! At the end of the meeting, there was an opportunity for those who wanted to give their lives to Jesus to come forward, and I couldn't help but make my way to the front. I was taken to the back of the church by a lady who spoke to me about what had happened. Crying, I told her I could feel God's incredible love for me and wanted to give my life to Him. She led me in a prayer, asking God to forgive me for my sins, and I asked Him to be my Lord and Saviour. I continued attending church with my family; however, my passion for God faded as I grew into my teens.

When I was nearly 20, my car was stolen. I had been the proud owner of it for only four months! I decided to use the money from the insurance to buy an open return ticket to England and hoped for an opportunity to visit Europe. I also envisaged obtaining some valuable work experience and then returning home afterwards. I felt alone and very far away from God. I didn't want to travel abroad but decided to because everyone my age was doing it. While standing at the top of the stairs leading into the aeroplane, I remember looking back with a sense of sadness at the Harare airport balcony (where people stood to wave goodbye to their loved ones), wondering when I would return. I called out quietly into the wind, "God, if You are there, will You reveal Yourself to me when I arrive in England?"

I arrived in London in August 1990, just after my 20th birthday and shared a room with my sister in a Christian hostel in Waterloo. I found it very difficult to adjust to the fast-paced life of London and to be honest, I hated it. I was often sick and had migraines regularly; it was the shock of being away from home. Having the open return ticket meant I could return any time within three months. However, I realised that achieving any of my goals would be impossible if I returned early. With a lot of courage, I tore up my ticket so I couldn't go back immediately and knew I would have to work to save up and buy another ticket. I applied for several jobs and accepted an offer for a permanent receptionist position.

I joined my sister's church in London but felt like a small fish in a massive ocean as the congregation was huge. There didn't seem to be anyone in my age group, though, and the lack of connection left me feeling even more distant from God. While living in the hostel, my sister decided to organise a Christmas concert, asking for volunteers to sign up to sing in the choir. Paul (my future husband from the Netherlands) was also living in the hostel and had signed up, and we met at the rehearsal. He was tall, slim and handsome, with blue eyes and a strong Dutch accent, and we seemed to have a lot in common. We were both Christians, our parents worried about us, and we were living in a country that wasn't our own. Paul soon realised that I could cook better than him, so most evenings, he would come into the girls' kitchen so that I could cook for him. Before we started dating, he shared with me a calling on his life to go to France as a missionary. Paul said that if I didn't feel I could go to live in France, he wouldn't date me. He did not want to fall in love with someone who would stop him from doing what he was called to do. It seemed like he was proposing to me on the first date, and I found it overwhelming! I had just started getting to know him and did not want to live in France, and I certainly didn't want to lose my Zimbabwean nationality; I was very proud of it.

Nevertheless, I wasn't going to tell him how I honestly felt. I simply said to him that going to live in France would be great. In the back of my mind, I thought, if we get married, I'll take you back to Zimbabwe. Not long after that, Paul invited me to his church; I loved being part of it, and the Bible teaching was excellent. I had made wonderful friends there, too, and my hunger for God had returned and increased. I knew the fire burning inside me to know God even more would not burn out this time, and I wanted to serve Him with all my heart. However, several months after dating Paul, he could see that I had a strong relationship with God, but he felt that I wasn't serious about going to France and that my family and country were more important to me. He gave me the weekend to think things over and to pray, but he seriously considered ending our relationship. I remember crying out to God to help me. I opened my Bible, desperately hoping something would jump out from the pages at me. My eyes fell across these verses:

"So Jesus answered and said, "Assuredly, I say to you, there is no one who has left house or brothers or sisters or father or mother or wife or children or lands, for My sake and the gospel's, who shall not receive a hundredfold now in this time—houses and brothers and sisters and mothers and children and lands, with persecutions—and in the age to come, eternal life." Mark 10:29-30 (NKJV)

I did not feel God was telling me I had to go to France, but I believed He was giving me a choice. As I had prayed for a Christian husband, I felt that Paul was my answer to prayer, and I did not want to lose him. I also knew that God had told me He would bless me. I realised that my life would be different from what I had initially thought (having my parents living nearby for when I would have children one day), but I knew that God would give us Christian friends, and we would be part of a large church family in France. The following day, I explained the revelation that I had to Paul. To cut a long story short, Paul proposed to me on the banks of the River Thames, and we married five months later in Zimbabwe.

Still living in London, Paul and I were in the process of preparing to move to France. I had begun to worry about whether I had what it takes to be a missionary. I heard God's audible voice for the second time just weeks before we left England. Again, feeling overwhelmed, afraid and unsure of what the future would hold, and wondering if I would cope with being so far away from my family in Zimbabwe, I awoke in the middle of the night hearing God say, "Do not be dismayed; I am with you." The room shook! Immediately after that, God showed me a vision of a little seven-year-old girl walking in the garden - and suddenly, I remembered and realised that it had been Him who had called me! I woke Paul up immediately, asking him if he had heard anything and was shocked to find that he hadn't! That same week, I received a letter from my mother, who was still in Zimbabwe; a letter would usually take ten days to two weeks to arrive. God had reminded her about it, too, and she wrote that she believed God had called me that day for this specific moment. This meant that He had reminded my Mum almost two weeks earlier than me so that her letter would arrive at the same time! I believe He wanted to put my mind at rest and confirm that He had called me as a missionary - that I didn't need to feel afraid for my future. God is such a wonderful, loving Father who never leaves us. He cares personally for each one of us. We don't need to worry about anything; we just need to trust Him that His plans for us are always good.

> *Psalm 23*
> *A psalm of David. The Lord is my shepherd; I have all that I need.*
> *He lets me rest in green meadows; he leads me beside peaceful streams.*
> *He renews my strength. He guides me along right paths, bringing honor to his name. Even when I walk through the darkest valley, I will not be afraid, for you are close beside me.*
> *Your rod and your staff protect and comfort me. You prepare a feast for me in the presence of my enemies. You honor me by anointing my head with oil. My cup overflows with blessings.*
> *Surely your goodness and unfailing love will pursue me all the days of my life, and I will live in the house of the Lord forever.*

To read about our 17-year season as missionaries in France, you can obtain a copy of my book, "*Beyond Our Limits. Faith Does Receive The Impossible.*" from Amazon.

CHAPTER 2

"Is It God Speaking?" "How Can We Recognise His Voice?"

"If you can't get a Word from God, Get Into The Word of God"
Pastor Vlad

HOW I BELIEVE GOD Speaks To Us And How We Can Discern His Voice:

There are several different ways in which I have experienced God speaking to me:

- Through His Word
- Through the Prophetic (Words of Knowledge, Words of Wisdom, Personal Prophecy)
- Through Teachers/Pastors/Evangelists (godly council) - *"Where no counsel is, the people fall: but in the multitude of counsellors there is safety."* Proverbs 11:14
- Through His Audible Voice

- Through the Holy Spirit
- In Dreams
- My Conscience Speaking

1. God speaks deep within my spirit. Satan speaks to my soul or mind. God alone resides within our spirit. God and Satan cannot both occupy our spirit man at one time. ("But he who is joined to the Lord becomes one spirit with him." 1 Corinthians 6:17).
2. God's voice is gentle and persuasive, free from pressure. Satan is loud and clamouring, always demanding an immediate response.
3. God's voice produces peace and a sense that everything is under control. Satan's voice speaks of despair; you have missed it; all is lost...
4. God's voice is always clear and distinctive, giving us a clear direction in which to go. The voice of Satan perplexes, causes confusion, loss of direction...
5. God tends to speak when I am seeking and listening. Satan breaks into our thoughts uninvited. (*"You will seek me and find me when you seek me with all your heart."* Jeremiah 29:13).

6. God says, "This is what you ought to do." Satan, or our own self-will screams, this is what you HAVE to do.

Ways God Speaks/Directs You:

He Gives You Peace: "*Let the peace of Christ rule in your hearts, to which indeed you were called in one body, and be thankful.*" (Colossians 3:15).

Confirmation: "*But he backs the word of his servant and confirms the counsel of his messengers. He says to Jerusalem, "Be inhabited," and to the cities of Judah, "Be rebuilt," and to the ruins, "I raise you up.*" (Isaiah 44:26)

Circumstances/Timing "*After these things Paul departed from Athens and went to Corinth. And he found a certain Jew named Aquila, born in Pontus, who had recently come from Italy with his wife Priscilla (because Claudius had commanded all the Jews to depart from Rome); and he came to them. So, because he was of the same trade, he stayed with them and worked; for by occupation they were tentmakers.*" (Acts 18:1-3)

This relationship between Paul, Aquila and Priscilla - which happened as a result of circumstances - became one of the most important strategic partnerships in the Book of Acts.

Building You Up/Encouragement: *"And now [brethren], I commit you to God [I deposit you in His charge, entrusting you to His protection and care]. And I commend you to the Word of His grace [to the commands and counsels and promises of His unmerited favor]. It is able to build you up and to give you [your rightful] inheritance among all God's set-apart ones (those consecrated, purified, and transformed of soul).*
(Acts 20:32)

Discipline: *"They disciplined us for a little while as they thought best; but God disciplines us for our good, in order that we may share in his holiness. No discipline seems pleasant at the time, but painful. Later on, however, it produces a harvest of righteousness and peace for those who have been trained by it."*
(Hebrews 12:10-11)

Warning You: *"Be very careful, then, how you live—not as unwise but as wise, making the most of every opportunity, because the days are evil."*
(Ephesians 5:15-16)

Requiring You To Die To Self: *"We know that our old sinful selves were crucified with Christ so that sin might lose its power in our lives. We are no longer slaves to sin."*
(Romans 6:6)

CHAPTER 3

Ice Cream Anyone?

"Life is good, especially on a Friday!"

I REALLY ENJOY FRIDAYS; somehow, they just feel different from other days. As a busy mum with four children close in age, I am beyond blessed! We had just moved to the UK, having lived in France for 17 years, and had joined a great church in Surrey where we could make friends and be involved in the community. Our children had started to go to our church youth club and always looked forward to going on Friday evenings. Weekends were busier than weekdays as we were taxiing them to different events, some in opposite directions. We were also very involved in helping out at our church. On Fridays after school, I would rush home to give my children a quick meal before dashing out again. I always felt sorry for our youngest son as he wasn't old enough to be able to go. After dropping the others off, he would be left sitting quietly by himself at the back of our 7-seater Ford Galaxy as we travelled back home again.

One Friday evening, I decided to treat him to an ice cream so that he would feel special while he waited for the others to return. "Joshua, we're going to take you out for a treat tonight to McDonald's so that you can have an ice cream." "I don't like their ice creams," he said (sorry, McDonald's 😊). He asked me if we could buy him a Cadbury's Dairy Milk ice cream instead. We decided to take him to Tesco to buy one there. He was happy but begged us not to go shopping; he really didn't like it when we went shopping. I promised we wouldn't; however, we remembered that the supermarket didn't only sell food but also sold other household goods. As I mentioned, we had only been in England for a short time and needed some dining room chairs, so we asked Joshua if he would mind if we quickly went up the escalator to see if they had any for sale. Thankfully, to his delight, they didn't, so we immediately took the escalator back down again. We went to the freezer section to look for his favourite ice cream and hunted high and low in all the freezers, including the special offer freezers at the end of each aisle. We couldn't find them anywhere, and he was very disappointed. We then spent the next ten minutes trying to find an alternative. He finally chose something, but the excitement had faded, and we made our way to the till, unaware of what would happen next.

CHAPTER 4

Helen and an Encounter With the Holy Spirit

"Some people come in
our life as blessings.
Some come in
your life as lessons."
Mother Teresa

WE LOOKED FOR THE till with the fewest people queueing and found one with only one person ahead of us. While waiting, I noticed that the lady ahead of us was scarily thin; her face was weathered, and her eyes were expressionless. On the conveyor belt in front of her was a bag of frozen broccoli, a tub of cream cheese and a large bottle of Vodka. It was a distressing sight, and I felt overwhelmed looking at her. Suddenly, I felt a prompting from the Holy Spirit. "Tell her that I love her." "What??" I said in my spirit. "Lord, is that You?" "Are You telling me to speak to her?" I heard it again. "Tell her that I love her."

All sorts of questions were buzzing in my head. "Why ME?!!" "What will she say?" "How will she react?" "Maybe she'll hit me over the head with her bottle of Vodka!" I felt terrified, but at the same time, I somehow also experienced a strange peace in my soul. I motioned to Paul and Joshua to come close to me and quietly spoke to them in French, so she wouldn't understand. "I feel God wants me to tell this lady something," I said. "You go on ahead, and I'll meet you in the car." I paid for the ice creams and passed them over to my husband, and they quickly escaped. As the lady was so weak, she was still struggling to pick up the few items that she had bought. I waited for her. As she headed slowly towards the exit, I walked alongside her. Then I did something unthinkable!! I put my arm around her bony shoulders and said, "God loves you." She looked a little startled as I told her I had never done that before; it wasn't like me to put my arm around a stranger like that! I then spluttered out again, "But God does love you!" She stopped walking and turned slowly to face me, and I took my arm away. "Does He *really* love me?" she asked. I explained to her again that I had never done anything like that before but had genuinely heard in my spirit that God wanted me to tell her that He loved her.

SPREADING GOD'S WORD BY TELLING YOUR STORY

Tears welled up in her eyes. I put my hand gently on her shoulder. "What's your name?" "Helen." "Helen," I said, "What a beautiful name." "It's so lovely to meet you; my name is Gaynor." "My husband and son are waiting for me in the car, and I'm sorry, but I'm going to have to dash now. Would you like us to continue this conversation another time?" She nodded. I asked for her phone number and searched for my mobile phone in my handbag. Phew! I found it! I added her name as a new contact and entered the numbers as she gave them to me. I read them out slowly, making sure I had done it correctly. "Let me call it to ensure it works," I said. I honestly thought she had given me the wrong number and didn't want to meet up with me again, but astonishingly, it was correct! I was so surprised when it rang. I told her I would be in contact soon, touched her gently on the shoulder again and walked out of the shop, turning briefly to wave goodbye. Wow! I couldn't quite believe what had just happened. My heart was pounding in my chest as I walked back to the car.

It was the end of spring, and I could still feel a nip in the air. It was getting dark, and I shivered a little as I scrambled into the car. My husband looked at me, and we stared for a moment at each other without saying anything. We both had been processing what we had just seen and experienced. He handed me an ice cream, but I didn't feel like eating it. We sat quietly for a bit, and then I finally broke the silence. I wanted to tell them everything that had happened, ensuring I didn't leave any details out. I talked about how we had gone to Tesco instead of McDonald's and had gone up the escalators to see if there were any dining room chairs. Then there was the hunt for the ice creams and the time it took to search for the next best option. After that, we arrived at the till, finding one person in front of us - Helen. I then concluded that she had given me her mobile phone number. I turned to my husband again and said, "Do you know, I believe that God delayed us getting to the till just so that we could be there at that perfect moment to meet her?!" I could feel goosebumps all over my arms, recounting what had happened.

We finished our ice creams in silence, and then Paul started the engine, and we made our way out of the car park. It was dusk, and the traffic had eased as most people were home by then. We finally reached the A3 and were nearing our home when we drove past some bare fields ploughed a few weeks before. I stared at the fields, eerily lit up by the street lights. Suddenly, a smell as sweet as roses on an early summer morning flooded the car. Joshua piped up, "Mum!" "Mum?" "Mum, what's that smell?" Paul and I looked at each other, knowing without a doubt what that fragrance was, even though we had never experienced it before. It was overwhelming! The fields were bare, and there could be no other explanation for the beautiful aroma that filled the air; it was the manifest presence of the Holy Spirit right there with us in the car! "Joshua," I said, "it's the fragrance of the presence of the Holy Spirit." Obeying God's prompting to speak to Helen had opened the door for us to experience the presence of the Holy Spirit in a new and unexpected way. I had read the Bible verse many times, which mentions "the fragrance of Christ", but this was the first time I had ever experienced it. We remained silent for the rest of the journey.

"For we are to God the fragrance of Christ among those who are being saved and among those who are perishing." 2 Corinthians 2:15

CHAPTER 5

Our Second Meeting

"We fear the future because
we are wasting today."
Mother Teresa

I WOKE UP AND went to make a cup of tea. What I had experienced felt like some sort of dream. I called Paul to come and have breakfast with me, and, feeling slightly uneasy, started to talk to him about Helen, knowing that she would be expecting a call from me at some point. "I don't know what to talk to her about when I call," I said. "What will I say?" "How can I help her?" "Oh, why did God get me involved?!"

Paul was always so wise. "Ask her this question when you call her...". "If there is one thing that you could ask God to do for you, what would it be?" I phoned her when I thought she would be out of bed. She answered pretty quickly in a quiet and timid voice. "Hello?" "Hi Helen, it's Gaynor, the lady you spoke to in Tesco on Friday." I asked how she was doing and if she had anything planned for the day. Thankfully, I find it relatively easy talking to people that I don't know well. I think it's because when I was at primary school, my teacher moved me from desk to desk, trying to stop me from talking in class. He would place me next to different pupils each lesson, but "miss chatterbox" continued, which gave me plenty of practice talking to others.

The moment came for me to ask Helen the question. She repeated it quietly, "If I could ask God one thing... um..." She thought for a while and said, "If I could ask God... I'd ask Him to keep me from losing my driving licence." She then brushed aside her comment and told me it was a long story. I suggested that it would be good to meet up and offered to take her out for lunch the following day. I had spoken to a few close friends about Helen at church and had mentioned that I was hoping to take her out for lunch. They thought she might want to go somewhere inconspicuous and didn't think she would appreciate eating out at our church café. I suggested a few pubs in the area but did mention the church café, where they served delicious soups or toasted sandwiches so that she had a choice. To my surprise, she chose to go to the church café!

The following day, I prayed before fetching her, asking God to help me give her some guidance. I felt nervous driving to her home and could feel my heart thumping in my chest. Helen had been watching out of the window for me, and as I drove up to her apartment, she gingerly made her way down the stairs to the car. I went to hug her; her bony frame troubled me. I opened the passenger door and helped her in, passing her the seatbelt. Once back in the car, I started to chat with her while driving, and she was surprisingly easy to talk to. When we arrived at the church café, we entered and found a table tucked away in the corner of the room. Helen ordered a packet of ready-salted crisps, a vegetarian sandwich, and a bottle of water. I desperately wanted her to order the most substantial meal on the menu and to eat until she was full. I ordered a toasted panini sandwich with smashed avocado and chicken and hungrily ate mine, but Helen barely touched what was on her plate. She looked disinterestedly at her food and pushed it gently to one side with her knife. Needing to find something to break the silence, I asked her a bit about herself, her hobbies, and where she had travelled. She used to be a hairdresser, loved "dolling people up," and was a brilliant painter - she showed me some photos on her phone of some of the fantastic paintings she had made. She had so many talents. As she talked to me about what she used to enjoy doing, I could see a slight sparkle appear in her eyes.

We talked casually about what she was currently doing, and she told me she was working at a shop in Surbiton. Suddenly, with a look of fear in her eyes, she asked, "Gaynor, do you remember that I told you that I would ask God to help me keep my driving licence?" "Well," she explained, "I was desperately depressed and had taken an overdose." "Without really knowing what I was doing, I went to my car and tried to drive it and immediately crashed into a parked car on my street." "I badly damaged my car and the one that I had driven into." Then she broke down. "I'm terrified they're going to take my driving licence away." "Who?" I asked. "Who's going to take your driving licence away?" "The DVLA," she said. "If they take my licence, I will not be able to drive to work, and I will lose my job." She then sobbed. "Helen," I said softly, "I don't believe that God would have stopped me in Tesco and asked me to speak to you if He wasn't able to deal with this." "I don't believe you'll lose it," I said. I believed that God was going to do a miracle for her. I felt that I needed to pray for her situation right then and there, and so I prayed, asking God for favour with the DVLA, that she would keep her licence and that her job wouldn't be affected. After praying, she looked a lot more peaceful. It was as if a huge burden had fallen off her shoulders. She managed a smile.

Helen continued to push her food around the plate and blushed, apologising for having ordered so much as she wasn't hungry. It really was a sad sight. I longed for her to eat what was on her plate, but I called the waitress and asked her if it was possible to pack the food into a bag so she could take it home.

SPREADING GOD'S WORD BY TELLING YOUR STORY

I felt I had said enough to Helen; she looked very drained, so I told her I would take her home to rest. She reached for her unopened packet of crisps and put them into her handbag.

I sent her a text every day with a Bible verse to encourage her and to find out how she was doing during the week, and the following Monday, I took her back to the church café. She loved being there so much and felt comfortable around people from our church. She spoke to me again about how much she regretted the mistakes that she had made. She knew she had hit rock bottom and felt so disillusioned with life. "It is clear that as you have hit rock bottom, there is only one way to go now, and that is up." "You can't go any further down." "All you have to do now is to turn around and start making the right choices for your life." "However, I believe it is impossible to do life without God's help." Using my phone, I showed her the famous painting by William Holman Hunt of Jesus standing at the door and knocking. I explained that the door had no handle on the outside, but it was up to the person inside to open it and let Jesus into their heart. "Do you want to ask Jesus to come into your life and to forgive you?" "He will help you to live your life the right way so that you will have peace and joy and be full of hope once again." "He will help you by giving you wisdom for your future." "Yes," she said. I asked her to pray after me, and she invited Jesus into her life to be her Lord and

Saviour, asking Him for forgiveness. It was such a special and amazing moment. It was surreal to think that the person I had met only two weeks previously was sitting opposite me and had just made the best possible decision she could ever make! I read one of my favourite verses from the Bible to her:

> *"In the same way, I tell you, there is rejoicing in the presence of the angels of God over one sinner who repents." Luke 15:10*

"Helen," I said, "the angels are now celebrating in heaven because of this amazing decision you have made!"

The following Monday, we met and discussed the possibility of her being able to do hairdressing and painting - to dream again, doing the things she loved most. She loved making people look beautiful by doing their hair. I envisage her getting stronger, being filled with joy and having a purpose in life. I could also imagine her standing on the stage at church one day, giving her testimony of what God had done. She would have an amazing testimony explaining how she had encountered Jesus and how He had transformed her life from being at "rock bottom" to being abundantly blessed and able to use all her gifts. She could live with the assurance that Jesus was with her every day and she wouldn't be alone anymore.

As Helen had been through so much for so long, it was evident that things wouldn't all immediately come right. She needed a lot of support. Some days, she struggled enormously, but I could tell she was grateful that she had found a friend she could confide in. I could see a hint of hope in her eyes that her situation would improve. She was extremely relieved that she had a friend who didn't judge her and still wanted to spend time with her even though she had taken drugs and her life was in a mess. I met with Helen every Monday for five weeks until it was time for my family's holiday abroad. I told her that I would keep in touch with her when I could and that she could text me whenever she wanted to, but I couldn't guarantee that I would have internet access throughout the day. I regretted leaving her as I knew it was early days for her, and she needed someone nearby she could call on.

When I could, I sent her a text. She responded initially, but gradually, towards the end of the first week of our holiday, her texts faded out, and she stopped replying. I was concerned, but knowing that I had only one week remaining of my holiday, I believed I could help her when I returned. I decided I needed to focus on enjoying my time away with my family and not worrying about her, but I sent her brief daily messages to let her know I was thinking of her.

CHAPTER 6

The Unexpected

"Some things are so unexpected that no one is prepared for them."
Leo Rosten

WE RETURNED LATE ON a Saturday evening from our sun-filled holiday and climbed into bed as soon as possible. The following day, we went to church, and throughout the service, I kept thinking about Helen. As soon as it was over, I told my husband that I felt I urgently needed to go to her apartment to see her. We gathered the children together and drove there. Paul stayed in the car with the children, and I went and rang the doorbell, not knowing what to expect. A man answered the intercom. "Hello, who is that?" I responded that I was a friend of Helen's whilst motioning to Paul to come to my aid. I knew that Helen lived alone and didn't have a boyfriend, so I was surprised that a man was answering her intercom.

The man came downstairs to meet us, shook our hands and introduced himself as Helen's brother. "You had better come upstairs," he said. Once in the apartment, we introduced ourselves again, and I told him briefly how I had come to know his sister. He started to speak, and his bottom lip trembled. "Helen committed suicide yesterday morning, and I have just come to sort things out. I live in Spain..." I was dumbstruck. I was surprised that I didn't faint, as it came as such a shock that words failed me! Tears rolled down my face... "and you won't believe it," he continued, "she was so terrified that she would lose her driving licence, but yesterday, just after she died, a letter arrived from the DVLA. It mentioned that her driving licence would be reinstated!"

Helen's brother didn't know anything about the prayers that I had been praying with her relating to her licence, but the Holy Spirit knew, and He wanted me to see that He had been working and had answered our prayers. I told him that I was a Christian and that Helen had given her life to Jesus before dying. It was a huge relief to him, but we were obviously devastated that she had decided she couldn't deal with life anymore. Looking at it now, I believe God knew that she would take her life. He had called on me at that vital moment because He loved her so much and wanted her to go to heaven. I was so relieved that I had obeyed. I knew all too well that if I had chosen to give in to my feelings of fear that day, she wouldn't have had the opportunity to give her life to God. I could easily have ignored God and gone home without talking to her!

"For this is how God loved the world: He gave his one and only Son, so that everyone who believes in him will not perish but have eternal life." John 3:16

Her brother took my details and promised to let me know when the funeral would be. We said goodbye and went back to the car. The children had been waiting patiently but could see by the looks on our faces that there was something seriously wrong. "What's happened?" Deborah piped up. "Helen committed suicide yesterday." I sobbed all the way home. I was devastated. Ten days later, I had a text from Helen's brother letting me know the details of the funeral. I was surprised at how rapidly his family had been able to organise it.

The day arrived to go to the crematorium, and I felt very nervous. I knew that I wouldn't know anyone at the funeral, but I prayed that I would be able to comfort those that I met. The little chapel was packed. People were standing against the walls on either side, while others were also standing at the back. Some of her colleagues had come to pay their respects. I tried to be brave, but I could hear sniffing and sobbing intermittently, and a lady in front of me suddenly started to cry profusely. I leant forward and gave her the spare packet of tissues I had brought; I knew they would be helpful. I couldn't hold back the tears anymore; why did I have to anyway? It was so desperately sad, but, thankfully, I can say "but," there is a happy ending... I know that I will see Helen again. She gave her life to Jesus, and I have no doubt that she is in heaven.

The funeral service ended, and we all walked slowly and quietly into the bright sunshine. White flowers, displayed in Helen's name, had been laid in the flower bed next to the trellis, which gave some shade from the sun. Her friends and relatives made their way towards them as if drawn by a magnet. A lady in a wheelchair was being pushed towards the flowerbed; I recognised who she was. It was Helen's mum. Helen was the splitting image of her mother. I made my way towards her and held her frail hand. How terrible it must be for a mother to have to bury her own daughter! I looked into her sad eyes and said, "You don't know me; my name is Gaynor." "I just want to say how sorry I am that Helen is not with us anymore." Her thumb gently stroked my hand as I was talking to her. I explained that I had met Helen a few months previously and that she had impacted my life. I told her that I had been able to lead Helen to Jesus and that she had given her life to Him. She smiled. She was such a lovely, gracious lady! Seeing hope restored on her wrinkled, drawn face was so wonderful. I gently stroked her shoulder and told her I was praying for her whole family. I then excused myself and made my way to speak to some other people.

I bumped into the lady that had been crying in front of me. She told me that she was Helen's neighbour and that she and her husband regretted terribly not being able to stop Helen from taking her life. Again, I explained how I had met Helen and that she had given her life to Jesus. I will never forget the relief on that lady's face! She told me that she was a Christian too and that they had known Helen for several years but didn't know how to help her. She was so thankful and told me she could be at peace, having the assurance that she would see Helen again one day. Looking back at the events of the day, I was amazed at how God continued to use me to speak to several people at the funeral, bringing them comfort by telling my story and hers. It gave them hope, knowing that if they gave their lives to Jesus, they would be able to see Helen again one day, too, but most importantly, they would meet with their Saviour Jesus!

CHAPTER 7

Charlotte

"A true friend accepts who you are, but also helps you become who you should be."

Fear of rejection stole my voice

WHEN I WAS 17 YEARS old and at a secretarial college in Harare, Zimbabwe, I had a special friend called Charlotte. We got on like a house on fire. Charlotte was tall with pretty blonde, short curly hair and huge blue eyes. She had the most incredible sense of humour and made me laugh a lot. A few years before I met her, she had had a brain haemorrhage, which left her temporarily unable to walk or talk. Thankfully, with specialist rehabilitation, Charlotte was able to return to school. Everything came back to normal apart from a limp - she dragged her right foot a bit when she walked, and she had epilepsy, which developed after the haemorrhage. Charlotte blamed God for her health challenges and her parents' divorce. She knew that I was a Christian, but she didn't ever want me to talk about my faith. It seemed to irritate her, and regrettably, I stopped talking about it because I was afraid of being rejected by her and losing our friendship.

One day, Charlotte's boyfriend had a car accident not far from where she lived. Thankfully, he was unhurt. Unfortunately, he had to stop on a blind corner when the traffic had come to a standstill. A car descending the hill at great speed towards him could not see what was ahead and ploughed into the back of his trailer. He phoned to tell her what had happened and she decided to walk from her home to the scene of the accident to see if she could help in any way. When she arrived, she went to inspect the damaged trailer and was standing between the trailer and her boyfriend's car when, at that very moment, another car came around the blind corner and crashed into the back of the vehicle that had caused the first accident. The impact forced the trailer to fly up into the air, and it careered into Charlotte, hitting her in the head and knocking her unconscious. Her boyfriend immediately called for an ambulance. The ambulance arrived shortly afterwards, and she was rushed to hospital. I was at work at the time and had a phone call to say that my friend was in intensive care. I asked my boss if I could leave work early so that I could go and visit her in the hospital. I cried out to God on the way there, "God, You helped her recover from the brain haemorrhage; please, will You help her recover from this too?" I was allowed into her room for just five minutes and was shocked to the core at what I saw, and I will never forget it! Her face was incredibly swollen, and her hands were battered and bruised. She was unconscious and looked so frightened! I prayed for her right there and then. When my time was up, I couldn't bear to leave her. I felt completely numb. I was unable to cry initially because of the extreme shock. I did not know how to process what had happened. How could such a freak accident have happened? After all she had been through, why had she succumbed to this? Why had this happened to *my* best friend? Would she be able to recover from this, too? I had no answers to my questions. I made my way home, hoping that I would soon wake up from my terrible nightmare. My Mum was looking out for me when I arrived. She held me and cried with me. Before sleeping that night, we prayed for her and her family. I struggled to get to sleep. For the next few days, my family decided to set aside a set time each evening to pray for her. We hoped that she would be able to survive this ordeal and make a full recovery.

Ten days later, I had to travel to Marondera (an hour's drive from Harare) to play my violin in an orchestral concert. After the concert, someone gave me a lift back to the College of Music in Harare, where my Mum was waiting to take me home. As I opened the boot of her car to put my violin inside, I noticed a stunningly beautiful flower arrangement my Mum had done. She was so talented in making flower arrangements. Looking at my Mum, I saw tears welling up in her eyes. She shook her head sorrowfully and then spoke softly, "I'm so sorry, Gaynor, but Charlotte died this morning, and I have brought these flowers so that we can take them to her family. I cried for weeks!! I missed my special friend so much, and I enormously regretted not talking to her about how much God loved her.

It was an opportunity that I had sorely missed with her. Much later on, I would discover that God would give me many other opportunities to speak to others about His love for them.

CHAPTER 8

Is This the End of the World?

"What the caterpillar calls
the end of the world,
the master calls a butterfly."
Richard Bach

The Unimaginable

IN MARCH 2020, THE UK government ordered the country into lockdown to try to stop the spread of COVID-19. I remember my son coming home from High School and telling me he would be home indefinitely. The dates of his GCSE examinations were fast approaching, and I didn't think he would be staying home longer than two weeks. Little did I know that it would end up being two years! He could not sit his GCSE examinations, so his final GCSE grades were awarded based on his mock examination results, which his teachers had approved. Thankfully, he had worked hard for them.

The news was mainly about people falling ill around us. Lockdown was especially difficult for me as I needed to be around people. It didn't seem to trouble my husband, who was used to working from home anyway. At the time, there were seven of us living under one roof. Our future daughter-in-law had arrived from France, and we did not know anyone in our church who wanted to take her in; they thought she could bring the virus into their home. We had no choice but to make room in our home to accommodate her. It was lovely getting to know her better. My family spent many evenings playing games and learning to appreciate one another. We were very thankful.

My daughters were studying at university then, and they hoped they wouldn't fall ill; they obviously did not want to miss any lectures. In November 2021, however, my eldest daughter contracted COVID-19. I didn't want to treat her like a leper, so I went into her bedroom and gave her a hug. The others weren't too keen for her to leave her room, but thankfully, none of us fell ill. Six weeks later, however, my youngest daughter returned from university feeling feverish and developed a cough the following day. I hugged her, too, but my husband and I contracted it then. Our children felt rough for a while but weren't very ill; however, I had a fever of 39 that was constant (it lasted for 16 days - I'll tell you more about what happened). I couldn't get the fever down, and the coughing was perpetual. My husband and I tried to do all we could to treat ourselves at home, including taking vitamins and paracetamol, using a nebuliser, checking our oxygen levels regularly with an oximeter and using an inhaler. We hadn't slept well for several days and lost our appetite. I had been vomiting, and my husband was spitting up blood, which was very scary. We also noticed that our oxygen levels were getting worse.

One morning, just a few days later, I can't begin to describe how ill my husband and I felt! My husband slid slowly out of bed and walked gingerly to his office to turn on his computer. He looked like a 90-year-old man shuffling down the corridor, and I was shocked to see how slowly he walked. I couldn't believe that he was going to attempt to work! I followed lethargically after him and told him that I wanted to check his oxygen levels before he did anything else. I put the oximeter on his finger, and it was 88%. Blood oxygen levels should usually be at 99% but not below 95%. As soon as I read out loud, "88%", he let out a huge groan and collapsed on his office chair. It was very alarming!

I quickly picked up my mobile phone and dialled 999. I spoke to the operator and told them that we both had Covid and that my husband had collapsed. As I was talking to her, I collapsed onto the floor. The operator called out, "Hello caller, hello caller, stay with me..." "Hello, caller?!!" As she was calling out, my husband woke up, picked up my mobile phone lying on his desk, and tried to talk to her. I then came round and realised I was on the floor. As I had initially made the emergency call, I took the phone out of his hand and told the operator that she had been talking to me. She started to take more details, but as I tried to answer, I collapsed again and fell back into the recliner armchair just behind where I was standing. The operator called out again, "Hello caller, hello caller, stay with me." "Hello, caller?!!!" My husband then grabbed the phone, and I remained in the chair. I didn't have an ounce of strength left to get up. The ambulance arrived ten minutes after our first call. It was incredible how quickly they were able to get to us. They examined us both, confirmed that we were doing the right things, and decided to leave us at home to look after ourselves as before, which I found pretty shocking! Just before leaving our house, they told me that should my husband collapse again, I was to roll him onto his side.

The following morning, I awoke exhausted from a terrible night's sleep as I had been coughing non-stop. I couldn't lie down at all during the night as my throat would block up with thick, sticky mucus, and I found it easier to breathe sitting up. My husband wanted to get out of bed, but I asked him to sit up first so that I could do a test to see how his oxygen levels were doing. I put the oximeter on his finger, and it read 88%. As soon as I read it out, he let out a huge groan again and collapsed back onto the hard wooden headboard of our bed. Remembering what the ambulance crew had told me, I tried desperately to turn him onto his side. It was impossible; I didn't know my oxygen levels weren't good either. If I had been 100% well, I know I would have struggled to get him onto his side anyway, as trying to move a dead weight is extremely difficult. As I was lacking oxygen, it was futile trying to turn him onto his side. Again I called for an ambulance, but this time I forgot to mention that I was ill too! Once again, they arrived within ten minutes. It was a different crew this time. They examined my husband again and decided that as the paramedics had visited the previous day, it was best to take him to the hospital and put him under observation. They guided him slowly down the stairs and left. My youngest daughter came up the stairs a short time later to check on me. She put the oximeter on my finger, and it read 88%. "Mum," she said, "I'm going to call an ambulance as your oxygen levels are too low." She phoned 999, but this time, they told her they didn't have any ambulances left to send and asked if anyone in the house could take me to the hospital. Thankfully, as my eldest daughter had already contracted the virus six weeks previously, she was able to take me.

I arrived at the hospital, and the nurse took me to a large open room for examination. I recognised my husband's voice, just around the corner from me. I phoned him briefly to let him know I was there too. Four members of staff buzzed around me. I was immediately given a nasal cannula, which provided supplemental oxygen, as my levels were still at 88%. I could not stop coughing and felt so sorry for the staff. I could see them flinching each time I coughed. The doctor ran off for a second face mask and a visor for extra protection. After several examinations, they decided my husband and I would stay overnight for observation. They told us there was no such thing as a ward for husbands and wives, so they separated us, but we were still on the same floor. They discovered that we both had pneumonia. I was also very dehydrated as I had been coughing for more than ten days.

I was wheeled to my room and put on a drip. The elderly lady opposite me wasn't doing well mentally. She muttered constantly and often called the nurses, and I just wanted it to be quiet in the room. Five other ladies shared the room with me, and four of them were on ventilators. As my bed was next to the window, I thankfully didn't have anyone next to me on my left-hand side. On my right was a lady called Maria from Lithuania; she was in her 40s and had moved to the UK not long before. She had been in hospital for over ten days and was looking extremely unwell. As I mentioned, I had a constant high fever lasting 16 days. During that time, I had to change my pyjamas twice daily, drenched from perspiration - the washing machine was on constantly. The day I went into the hospital, I was wearing the last and worst pair of clean but ill-fitting pyjamas that I had left in my drawer. I obviously wasn't wearing makeup and hadn't brushed my hair. I looked dreadful!

Maria introduced herself to me. We talked briefly about our families, and I told her, in between a lot of coughing, that I had four children. "How old are you?" she asked. "51," I said. "You look SO young!" I tried to smile. We talked periodically; her coughing seemed more in control than mine. A few hours later, again, she said, "You look so young for your age!" It didn't make sense - I would have easily agreed with her if she had said, "You look so ill." I slept on and off when I could, only too aware of the coughing, while my exhausted body tried to switch off. The nurse came several times during the day to check on me and to see if my fever was going down. The staff were so kind. I FaceTimed my husband just to see him; I knew we wouldn't be able to talk much. He cried as he wasn't sure if he would make it out alive. We both weren't! I looked at Maria and said, "I've just called my husband, who is also here in the Covid ward." "He looks awful!" She pursed her lips. "I know I have said this twice already," she said, "but you really do look young for your age!"

Suddenly, it hit me! My husband and I had many people praying for us in South Africa, Zimbabwe, Australia, New Zealand, France, the USA and the

UK! "She must be sensing the Holy Spirit," I thought. I felt goosebumps all over my arms. "It must be that!" Without knowing it, I had been reflecting "the glory of the Lord", and she sensed His presence in the room.

> *"For the Lord is the Spirit, and wherever the Spirit of the Lord is, there is freedom. So all of us who have had that veil removed can see and reflect the glory of the Lord. And the Lord— who is the Spirit—makes us more and more like him as we are changed into his glorious image."*
> 2 Corinthians 3:17-18

It was incredible how the Holy Spirit had suddenly changed my focus from thinking about myself and how I felt, to "seeing" what I could do to help those in my room as if I had had a "veil removed" from my eyes.

"My husband and I are Christians, and many people are praying for us," I said. "I think you keep saying that I look young because you may be sensing that people are praying for us." (I knew it was because of the presence of the Holy Spirit, but I worded it that way so that she would not feel uncomfortable). "I have also realised that you probably don't have anyone praying for you right now; is that right?" "Yes, and I am probably going to die here, and I don't know who is going to look after my heavily autistic 15-year-old son." "No, Maria," I said, "don't say that again." "I really believe that God has placed me in this room so that I can pray for us all, and I believe that we are all going to get out of here alive." "Would you like me to pray for you?" "Yes, please," she said. Filled with faith, I said, "I'm going to pray for a huge miracle for you." "I'm going to ask God to make you well enough so that you can be home for Christmas, and you'll be able to be with your son." Looking at her current state, I knew that only God could do that, and I knew I was believing for something that seemed impossible! Maria had mentioned that she was a Catholic, so I didn't think she would refuse my offer to pray for her.

Lying opposite us was a lady called Carol. I knew she had heard every word we had been saying, and honestly, I wanted her to. Carol was strapped in and constantly turned by a specialised mechanical bed used to improve her breathing. Like Maria, she was also on a ventilator. She was very ill and had been in hospital for several days; her situation looked bleak. "Carol," I said, "you must have heard my conversation with Maria." "Would you like me to pray for you too?" Carol shifted uneasily in her bed - I could tell she was not a churchgoer and wasn't comfortable hearing me talk about God. "You have nothing to lose, Carol." "Ok," she said. "I'm going to pray the same prayer that I prayed for Maria... that God will enable you to be home for Christmas." It was the 18th of December 2022, and I knew only seven days remained until Christmas Day. God would have to do something incredible to get them both home by then!

One of the nurses who had been looking after me was called Martha. "Martha," I said, "you were named so well!" I was thinking about the Bible story of Martha, who was busy preparing food for Jesus and His disciples. She smiled. "You must be the lady married to the man called Paul down the corridor." "Yes," I said. "You are both so funny - you seem to do everything together - going on a mission to France, and you even come to the hospital together on the same day!" I smiled and nodded.

Meanwhile, my husband had written a letter to one of his close friends at church, asking him to pass it on to me and our family should he die. While he was in his hospital room, he started to talk to a man who said he was afraid of dying and had been there for over three months with COVID-19. He had been in several motorbike accidents in the past, and his body had to fight extra hard to recover. Apparently, one could see the metal pins sticking out of his mangled legs. My husband told him that he believed that if he would die, he would go to heaven. The man said he hoped he would go there too but didn't yet have the conviction. The Bible says, *"I write these things to you who believe in the name of the Son of God so that you may know that you have eternal life."* (1 John 5:13). Paul explained to him how to become a Christian. He then prayed with him, and he gave his life to Jesus. When he had finished praying, the man said he was filled with peace and was no longer afraid to die. Praise God!

The following day, they sent us home. It took several weeks for us to recover fully. Maria gave me her number, and I texted her to find out how she was getting on. "Both Carol and I were out of hospital on Christmas Eve," she said. "God answered your prayers!" I thanked God for that amazing miracle!

Three months later, we returned to the hospital for a scan to check if our lungs had fully recovered. Thankfully, our lungs had, and there was no need for further checkups. I used to suffer a lot from hay fever during the summer months and used inhalers to help with my breathing. Amazingly, since contracting COVID-19, I have not needed to use my inhalers once, and I believe that God has restored my lungs to full health. They are now in better condition than they were before I fell ill. I am so thankful to Him!

I decided to share this story to show you how God can use a bad situation and turn it into something good for His glory. He changed our focus from being on ourselves and how ill we felt, to noticing that people around us are in desperate need of a Saviour and need physical and spiritual healing. He is awesome!!

CHAPTER 9

Sharing the Gospel Effectively

"Success is due to our stretching to the challenges of life. Failure comes when we shrink from them."
John C. Maxwell

The Miracle Is In The Stretch

SEVERAL YEARS AGO, WHEN my husband and I went to live in France as missionaries, our lovely Portuguese neighbour was the first person I met. As much as I wanted to share my faith with her, I found it more challenging to talk to her about it than about trivial matters. I felt awkward and inexperienced, but I pushed myself to speak to her about Jesus because I knew God wanted me to. It stretched me to get out of my comfort zone and increase my knowledge of Scripture so that I would be more comfortable sharing my faith with her and others. She was friends with some pastors we were working with, and they had tried to talk to her about God for a couple of years but didn't feel they had made any progress with her. They became frustrated and decided to move on, dedicating their time to others who were more open or ready to make that step. We, however, didn't believe it was right to give up on her just because she wasn't open to it at that moment. We continued building our friendship, meeting up for a coffee occasionally or having dinner with her family, and every year, I made her a birthday cake.

Ten years after I first met her, I showed her something I had bought online called the "EvangeCube", a seven-picture cube resembling a Rubik's cube. I bought it to make it easier to explain the Gospel when talking to people about Jesus. It was an excellent tool that increased my confidence when speaking to people about my faith.

I pulled the EvangeCube out of the box to show her and explained the meaning of the different images. She looked at me, absolutely stunned! "That is brilliant," she said. "The Gospel is so easily explained using this tool that now I understand why

SPREADING GOD'S WORD BY TELLING YOUR STORY

Jesus came to die for me." "I would like to give my life to Him right now." I prayed a very simple prayer with her, and she gave her life to Jesus. As I mentioned earlier, we had been friends with her for ten years before she was ready to make that life-changing decision, but we were so glad that we hadn't given up on her and that we had come across this tool that made it easier for her to understand! Stepping out of my comfort zone had stretched me, but an incredible miracle had taken place!

CHAPTER 10

The Stay-At-Home Christian

"Refuse to be a lazy Christian, and resist a passive, apathetic attitude." Joyce Meyer

"And let us not neglect our meeting together, as some people do, but encourage one another, especially now that the day of his return is drawing near." Hebrews 10:25

THERE ARE MANY REASONS why some Christians have decided not to attend church anymore. Since COVID-19, for example, some have decided to continue watching their church services online because they can stay in their pyjamas and don't have to make an effort to go out. Sadly, some churches had to close down, and some of their members, mostly the elderly, didn't want to go elsewhere or have become apathetic. For some, there isn't another church in the vicinity. Tragically, others were so filled with fear of contracting the virus that they were too afraid to return.

Other Christians have been deeply hurt by someone or something that happened in church and have vowed never to go back. Another reason could be that their pastor may have moved on, and they don't get on as well with the current one, or perhaps the pastor's teaching is Biblically unsound. Another category is those who have had to leave their countries. The trauma of leaving their churches, family and friends has pushed them into a corner where their joy has been sapped, and they don't have the motivation to find a new church family and make new friends. The list goes on. It is essential to shed light on these issues and to realise that it is up to each one of us to reach out to them, love them in whatever way possible - to help with transport if there is a need, to be a friend, and encourage them to come back into the community.

God has often led me to bump into Christians who fit into the above categories. I will often talk with them about the fact that we lived in France for 17 years before coming to England and that starting all over again was challenging. However, joining a lively church and being part of a loving community really helped us to settle. When I mention this, their eyes light up, and they ask more questions about where my church is based and want to know more. I encourage them to "come and see." More often than not, they soon find their place. We are to encourage our Christian brothers and sisters not to "neglect meeting together." To those who are hurting, I simply say that if I found a perfect church, it would no longer be perfect because I'm not perfect! They then understand that they can't continue to use that excuse to keep them away from what God has for them, and realise that they need to learn to forgive and move forward.

> *If you forgive those who sin against you, your heavenly Father will forgive you. But if you refuse to forgive others", your Father will not forgive your sins."* Matthew 6:14-15

The Bible clearly states that we can't be forgiven unless we forgive.

Jesus Taught Us How To Pray:
Now it came to pass, as He was praying in a certain place, when He ceased, that one of His disciples said to Him, "Lord, teach us to pray, as John also taught his disciples."
So He said to them, "When you pray, say:
Our Father in heaven,
Hallowed be Your name.
Your kingdom come.
Your will be done
On earth as it is in heaven.
Give us day by day our daily bread.
And forgive us our sins,

For we also forgive everyone who is indebted to us.
And do not lead us into temptation,
But deliver us from the evil one."
Luke 11:1-4

When Christians stay home instead of attending church and being part of the community, they lose their effectiveness and their voice. How can we help one another and learn from each other if we don't make an effort to meet together?

> *"As iron sharpens iron, so one person sharpens another."* Proverbs 27:17

We have been commissioned to get out of our comfort zone:

> *"He said to them, "Go into all the world and preach the gospel to all creation."* Mark 16:15

We need to leave the past behind, choose not to give into fear and start moving forward.

Pressing toward the Goal

> *"I don't mean to say that I have already achieved these things or that I have already reached perfection. But I press on to possess that perfection for which Christ Jesus first possessed me. No, dear brothers and sisters, I have not achieved it, but I focus on this one thing: Forgetting the past and looking forward to what lies ahead,"* Philippians 3:12-13

SPREADING GOD'S WORD BY TELLING YOUR STORY

Someone once said, "The only person who can stop you from reaching your goals is you." God has put something great inside each of us, which He wants us to accomplish for His glory, but we will not be able to achieve much if we stay at home or allow fear or unforgiveness to rule our lives.

Jesus Taught Us What To Pray:

But when He saw the multitudes, He was moved with compassion for them, because they were weary and scattered, like sheep having no shepherd. Then He said to His disciples, "The harvest truly is plentiful, but the labourers are few. Therefore pray the Lord of the harvest to send out labourers into His harvest." Matthew 9:35-38

God listens, speaks, and responds when we pray, and prayer moves the heart of God, and He moves mountains.

We are the labourers in our sphere of influence, so let's be willing to go out into the harvest.

CHAPTER 11

A Chip Off The Old Block

"Don't be content to be the chip off the old block - be the old block itself." Winston Churchill

MY MOTHER WAS SUCH a wonderful lady who loved Jesus wholeheartedly. She studied her Bible every day and did her best to memorise as many Scriptures as she could to use them at an opportune moment. Mum would share her faith with people whenever possible. Mum taught me everything she had learned about Jesus, and her ceiling became my floor. In other words, I would hopefully go beyond what she had learnt about God and move further on with Him.

One day, Mum told me about an interesting conversation with a Muslim taxi driver. She took the opportunity to talk to him about Jesus while he was driving her somewhere. "Who do you believe Jesus was?" she asked. " He was a very good man, a prophet," he replied. "Do you think good prophets lie?" she asked him. "No," came the response. "Well then, what did Jesus mean in John 14:6 when He said, *"I am the way, the truth, and the life. No one comes to the Father except through Me."*? He had never heard that before and told her he would go home and think about it some more. It was good food for thought.

When my mother was on her deathbed, she was still talking to people about Jesus. When I visited her in her hospital room, she was talking to a nurse about her faith in Jesus, and she was obviously very moved by what she had said. The nurse had had many challenges in her life. She was a single mum trying to provide for her family financially as well as emotionally, and it was evident how difficult life had become for her. My mother reassured her that even when she had felt alone, Jesus had always been with her. He wasn't the one who had created the problems, but He was there, ready to help her turn a bad situation into something good. It was amazing that as my mother talked with her, she became aware that God had indeed been with her during those difficult times.

The nurse shared with me what they had just been discussing and started to cry. It was tough for her to be showing her emotions in a professional environment, but I couldn't let the moment go by.

SPREADING GOD'S WORD BY TELLING YOUR STORY

"Have you given your life to Jesus?" I asked. "No," she replied. I asked if she would like to do that, and she eagerly nodded. I explained that Jesus would forgive her for her sins, and she would become His child. I then led her to pray a short prayer with me. After praying, the joy on her face was indescribable, and such a peace came over her tear-stained face. Without realising it, my Mum and I had worked together as a team to help this precious lady give her life to Jesus. You don't always have to talk to people alone - working with a friend can also be incredibly effective.

N.B. If you are at work, it is always best to share your faith with a colleague during your lunch break or after hours, as you shouldn't be proselytising during work hours.

CHAPTER 12

"O death, where is your victory?" "O death, where is your sting?"

"I truly never learned what the words "I miss you" were until I reached for my Mum's hand, and it wasn't there."

WE HAD JUST RETURNED from a fantastic holiday visiting our cousins in California. Knowing that my Mum was close to death, my cousin, who is a chaplain there, gave me a booklet to help prepare me called "Life After Loss - Grieving With Hope" by Tim Jackson. It begins by asking, "Is there such a thing as good grief?" Each time I tried to sit down and read it, something would distract me, and I'd put it back down again. Then, one day, my car developed a problem, and I had to take it to the garage. As I was leaving the house, I realised I would have a lot of time on my hands and could read the booklet while waiting, so I returned to get it. I left the car in the garage and walked a short distance to McDonald's to buy myself a coffee and read. As I walked in, I noticed it had recently been refurbished, and a lovely new leather sofa had been placed in a quiet spot. I decided to sit there. I took the booklet out and started to read it.

Two hours passed, and I only had a few pages to finish when my phone rang. I had forgotten that I was to expect a call from the garage as I had been so engrossed in reading it. I decided to finish it later that evening and quickly went to fetch my car, realising it was time to pick up my son from school. When I reached the school gates, my phone started to ring again. I quickly parked my car and saw that it was my Dad calling. "Hi Dad...?" "Gaynor, Mum's gone!" How do you ever prepare yourself for a phone call like that? I felt numb all over. Mum sadly had many health challenges in her lifetime, but for the remaining nine months of her life, she had suffered enormously, and we felt so helpless not being able to help her. My cousin had said that I would be hard hit by grief when she died. He knew my Mum well; he also knew just how much I loved her, and everyone who knew her loved her too. Strangely enough, I didn't cry when my Dad called.

I had such peace, and I can actually say that I was happy at that moment as I knew that her suffering was finally over.

When my son and I arrived home, I told the rest of the family and then phoned my cousin in California to tell him the sad news. I explained to him how God had prepared me for what was to come that afternoon by reminding me to read the booklet just hours before she died. Once again, he told me I would find it extremely hard, but I disagreed. "No," I said, "I know that Mum is in heaven now, and I can't begin to tell you how relieved I am for her that her pain and suffering are now over." "I know I will see her again, which gives me so much hope and peace." "I will be absolutely fine!"

Six weeks after my Mum died, the shops were getting ready for the Christmas season, and the Christmas lights were being put up in our village high street. I started to think about what Christmas would look like without my precious Mum. She loved baking and making gifts for people, especially for her family. She used to make spiced chutney, fudge and marshmallows, to name a few, as well as homemade pressed flower cards to give to people at church. She would spend her evenings crocheting colourful ponchos and blankets for children. I was thinking about all she used to do for everyone when, just out of the blue, I let out a huge groan and started to sob. I cried so uncontrollably that my husband, working in the upstairs office, came down to see what was happening. I think he thought at first that I had severely injured myself. I cried until I was exhausted. I lost my appetite and went straight to bed. The following day, I tried to go about my work, but a huge cloud of sadness enveloped me, and every time I thought about my Mum, which was very often during the day, I would cry.

I phoned my cousins in California; I was desperate to talk to them so that they could comfort me. "I don't know what to do," I said. "I have so much pain in my chest that I feel like a huge knife has just pierced my heart!" "That's because you loved her so much," they said. That statement reminded me of what a preacher once said, "The depth of your sorrow indicates the depth of your love." It was comforting when they told me I was "a very good" daughter. They knew that I would have no regrets as I had said everything I needed to say to my Mum before she died. I told her what an amazing mother she had been and thanked her for her devoted love to me and to my whole family. I apologised for the times I had let her down or had been unkind. I had read Bible verses to her and prayed for her often. Two hours before she died, a letter I had written to her and posted a few days previously had arrived just in time for my sister to read to her. I had written down several Bible verses that talked about heaven, and I told her that it was ok to go to heaven and that I would do my best to look after the rest of the family.

The pain of grief continued and was so intense that I finally came to the realisation that I was becoming a burden to my family. Life had to continue without my Mum, but my life had come to a standstill, and I didn't know how to do life without her. A friend encouraged me to contact a local charity that deals with bereavement counselling to see if they could help me. I realised that it wasn't fair on my husband to constantly remind him of how sad I was feeling (actually, he didn't need reminding as he could see how miserable I was every day!). He loved her too and had a special relationship with her, but I felt that the grief was creating a wedge between us, and I needed to sort it out.

The people at the bereavement charity were lovely. They arranged for someone to come and meet me. I was able to talk to one of their volunteers about my Mum and what a special lady she was. I talked about what I appreciated about her and what she used to do for my family and for others. I then started to share about my Mum's faith in Jesus and how she used to lead a Bible study group. She was very artistic and would write Bible verses in calligraphy on pressed flower cards to give to people on special occasions. The lady wasn't a Christian but was very interested in hearing what I had to say. I shared with her weekly about what I had learned at church the previous Sunday. It was so amazing that God had given me an opportunity to share my faith with her while she was helping me with my grief! It just came naturally to me. One Sunday, the sermon was life-changing for me. The preacher talked about the man at the pool of Bethesda:

> *After this there was a feast of the Jews, and Jesus went up to Jerusalem. Now there is in Jerusalem by the Sheep Gate a pool, which is called in Hebrew, Bethesda, having five porches. In these lay a great multitude of sick people, blind, lame, paralyzed, waiting for the moving of the water. For an angel went down at a certain time into the pool and stirred up the water; then whoever stepped in first, after the stirring of the water, was made well of whatever disease he had. Now a certain man was there who had an infirmity thirty-eight years. When Jesus saw him lying there, and knew that he already had been in that condition a long time, He said to him, "Do you want to be made well?"*
>
> *The sick man answered Him, "Sir, I have no man to put me into the pool when the water is stirred up; but while I am coming, another steps down before me."*
>
> *Jesus said to him, "Rise, take up your bed and walk." And immediately the man was made well, took up his bed, and walked.* John 5:1-8

When the counsellor arrived at my home the following day, I greeted her excitedly. "You look so much better today," she said. "What has happened?" I went to the kitchen to make her a cup of tea and

SPREADING GOD'S WORD BY TELLING YOUR STORY

told her to make herself comfortable in the lounge. "I had a sudden revelation on Sunday," I said. "I feel like I'm the one who has been lying at the pool of Bethesda all this time expecting someone else to lift me up and heal me, but I realise that I am the one who needs to make the decision and say to myself, "Right, Gaynor, you have grieved long enough now; you need to move on." She was amazed. She loved it when I shared things from the Bible with her. This time, though, she could see that something had dramatically changed in me. I was a different person. She came to check on me just a few more times, but I was strong again.

I invited her to our church's Christmas concert; she brought her whole family and loved it! I would never have thought it possible to share my faith with the lady who had come to help me! However, it's amazing how God turned the situation around. As she went out of her way to help me, I believe she was even more blessed.

> *Generosity brings prosperity, but withholding from charity brings poverty. Those who live to bless others will have blessings heaped upon them, and the one who pours out his life to pour out blessings will be saturated with favor.*
> Proverbs 11:24-25

Incredibly, even when things are not going well, God can still use us to bless others, sow seeds into their lives and bring them to Him through our challenges.

CHAPTER 13

Sharing Our Faith In Jesus

"There's only one thing
more precious than our time
and that's who we spend it on."
Leo Christopher

THE APOSTLE PAUL SHARED his faith with those in Jerusalem by quoting Scripture from memory. When he spoke to the people of Athens, however, who were from a pagan culture, he spoke differently to them so that they could understand that they worshipped false gods.

> Paul then stood up in the meeting of the Areopagus and said: "People of Athens! I see that in every way you are very religious. For as I walked around and looked carefully at your objects of worship, I even found an altar with this inscription: to an unknown god. So you are ignorant of the very thing you worship—and

this is what I am going to proclaim to you. Acts 17:22-23

We are living in a post-Christian era in the West, and many people are Biblically illiterate. Before sharing our faith, we need to take time to get to know the person by taking them out for a coffee, listening to them and asking questions. Getting to know them and showing that you care about them builds trust. You may have heard this expression, "People don't care how much you know until they know how much you care." If they have no Biblical background, it's a good idea to explain Genesis to them. They will then understand why Jesus came to earth. They may say things that you disagree with, but that's ok. Don't pull out the pulpit - in other words, don't use a religious voice when sharing a Bible verse with them. If they ask questions and you don't know the answer, that's ok too. Just respond that you will try to find out and will get back to them.

Here is the Gospel in just 30 seconds, which shows how simple it is to explain:

Adam was the first man that God created. Do you know that we're all descendants of Adam? Adam rebelled against God, and that's called sin. Do you know what happened? Because of that sin, death came into the world, and that's why we die. We have all sinned, and we're all going to die one day, but do you know what God did? He stepped into history to die on the cross. His name is Jesus. He was raised from the dead after three days and offers us a free gift of salvation. Repent, and you will be saved and will be with Him in heaven for eternity when you die.

Obviously, we don't want to rattle that off to someone just like that because it may put them off.

When reaching out to Generation Z - the generation born in the late 1990s or the early 21st century (perceived as being familiar with the use of digital technology, the Internet, and social media), we need to remember that, for the most part, they have not heard the Bible read in schools. They did not have to recite the Lord's Prayer in their assemblies or listen to prayers from the podium. They probably don't know anything about the Bible and have learned that everything is acceptable and permissible. They need to be taught right from the beginning. This generation is comparable to the Greeks in Acts 17, who worshipped many gods. The Greeks felt there was something out there that they were missing but didn't know what it was ("to an unknown god").

There is power in the message of the Life, Death and Resurrection of Jesus, and that is why the Apostle Paul said:

> *"For I am not ashamed of this Good News about Christ. It is the power of God at work, saving everyone who believes—the Jew first and also the Gentile."* Romans 1:16

The Apostle Peter spent time eating with people in their homes. He showed them that he cared and then presented the Gospel to them.

Soon the news reached the apostles and other believers in Judea that the Gentiles had received the word of God. But when Peter arrived back in Jerusalem, the Jewish believers criticized him. "You entered the home of Gentiles and even ate with them!" they said. Acts 11:1-3

Peter's message was effective because it was scriptural. He called sin "sin" and told them to repent. First of all, we need to define what sin is. It is falling short of a standard that God has set for humanity: perfection. We have all sinned. Sometimes, we are afraid to tell people that they have sinned.

Peter said,

"Let all the house of Israel therefore know for certain that God has made him both Lord and Christ, this Jesus whom you crucified." Now when they heard this they were cut to the heart, and said to Peter and the rest of the apostles, "Brothers, what shall we do?" And Peter said to them, "Repent and be baptized every one of you in the name of Jesus Christ for the forgiveness of your sins, and you will receive the gift of the Holy Spirit." Acts 2:36-38

The word "cut" means to stab, and it speaks of something sudden and unexpected - the conviction of the Holy Spirit.

We may be led to share something from the Bible that we know someone won't agree with. I believe, however, that God will enable us to share it in a non-condescending way. Do you think that you should stop quoting the Bible just because someone says that they don't believe in it? No. There is power in the Word of God; it is the "Sword of the Spirit". We must use the Word; keep it conversational. Scripture can sometimes be like a timebomb that detonates later. A person may act like they don't care, but then in the early hours of the morning, they wake up, and the verse that you shared with them will be in their head. God's Word will not return void.

> *As the rain and the snow come down from heaven, and do not return to it without watering the earth and making it bud and flourish, so that it yields seed for the sower and bread for the eater, so is my word that goes out from my mouth: It will not return to me empty, but will accomplish what I desire and achieve the purpose for which I sent it.* Isaiah 55:10-11

A 2020 survey from "Probe Ministries" in Relevantmagazine.com released a shocking statistic that "60% of born-again Christians under the age of 40 agree with the statement that "Jesus isn't the only way to Salvation", that "Buddha, Muhammad and Jesus are all valid paths to God." ("Survey: 60

Percent of Born-Again Christians Under 40 Say Jesus Isn't the Only Way to Salvation - RELEVANT")

This means that 60% of born-again Christians have not read their Bibles properly, or 60% of them think that they are born again. If you are a born-again Christian, you cannot believe that Buddha and Muhammad are equal to Jesus in getting you to heaven. Thinking about it logically, if it is true that all roads get you to heaven, why would God send His Son to suffer and die on the cross? He did it because there was no other way to satisfy His righteous demands. Jesus wasn't a guru or a prophet; He was God who became a man and walked among us. God sent His Son to die in our place so that we could be forgiven of our sins. Jesus said it very clearly:

> *"I am the way, the truth, and the life. No one comes to the Father except through Me."* John 14:6

Some of the reasons we don't evangelise are:

- Fear of rejection
- Not knowing how to do it
- Not being confident
- Being afraid of what people think of us
- It is not the right time or place
- We are afraid of being labelled as a Christian fanatic/Bible basher

SPREADING GOD'S WORD BY TELLING YOUR STORY

When a new believer asks us to clarify something, and we explain what the Bible teaches, it re-energises, excites and revives us in our walk of faith, and we can trust that the Holy Spirit will work in that person's heart in His own timing. It is not our job to convert people; we can't convert anyone. The work of conversion is done by the Lord; we just need to be His mouthpiece.

Jesus said,

> "The harvest is great, but the workers are few. So pray to the Lord who is in charge of the harvest; ask him to send more workers into his fields." Luke 10:2

> "No one can come to me unless the Father who sent me draws them, and I will raise them up at the last day. John 6:44

To summarise, we need to:
1. Get to know the person we are trying to reach
2. Quote Scripture
3. Call sin "sin" and tell them to repent, asking them if they want to accept Jesus, and then
4. Conversion is God's work; our job is to share the Gospel

A good way to remember how to share your faith is by using the acronym "BLAST".
- Build a bridge.

Start your conversation by building a bridge to your listener. You don't have to start by preaching to them.

- **Listen.**

Get to know them and take an interest in them.

- Ask questions to get to know them better.

Ask them what they enjoy doing, what their favourite holiday was, and simple things that encourage them to talk about themselves.

- Share your testimony

This is the bridge; it's one of the most effective ways to start your conversation by telling them what Jesus has done for you. If you have experienced the life-changing power of Jesus, then you can boldly share that experience with others. They may argue about the facts of the Gospel but cannot argue about your experience. They cannot argue about your testimony; it's your story.

- Tell them about Jesus.

When we put these principles into practice, we will see people coming to Jesus.

During the lockdowns, many people suffered from depression because they were isolated. Recently, I have found that when talking with non-Christians about the importance of community, they understand that being part of a church benefits one's mental health. They share about the fear they felt during COVID-19 and question more about the meaning of life now than before. They ask questions about whether there is a God that cares for our well-being when referring to the recent wars and the cost-of-living crisis. I believe that they are, therefore, more likely to accept an invitation to come to church.

In 2020, the most popular book was the Bible, and the Bible App's top verse globally was Isaiah 41:10 *"Fear not, for I am with you; Be not dismayed, for I am your God. I will strengthen you, Yes, I will help you, I will uphold you with My righteous right hand."* Fear has pushed people to look for something that would bring them peace. I have spoken to some people who have mentioned that they have started praying daily when this has not been their usual practice.

> *"But when you hear of wars and rumours of wars, do not be troubled; for such things must happen, but the end is not yet".* Mark 13:7

CHAPTER 14

Peace In Turmoil

"Peace is not just the absence of conflict; peace is the creation of an environment where all can flourish, regardless of race, colour, creed, religion, gender, class, caste, or any other social markers of difference."
Nelson Mandela

MANY YEARS AGO, MY husband and I worked for a charity called "The Green Light Project". Every Friday evening, we would walk through the dimly lit streets of Soho, the Red-Light District of London, to "The Alley Cats Coffee Bar". It was an unpleasant journey as we walked past prostitutes standing in their doorways, trying to coax men in. Once, a woman grabbed Paul's arm, trying to lure him in while I was holding onto him! I was always grateful when we reached our destination, could unlock the door, and let ourselves in.

The Coffee Bar was a room with a built-in kitchen where young, homeless people from around London would come to have a free hot meal and to chat with someone they felt safe with. A team of men and women from our church went weekly to help. We met all sorts of homeless people - some were alcoholics, drug addicts, punks, prostitutes, a few came from other countries, both male and female. They would briefly escape their freezing cardboard shelters and dangerous surroundings for a few hours just to have a safe haven. Dinner was usually a baked potato with some filling and lashings of grated cheddar cheese with coleslaw on the side. You could "feel" them shivering as they hungrily ate their steaming potatoes. Coming from a secure and supportive family background, I couldn't begin to identify with their lifestyle of living in cardboard boxes, makeshift tents and filthy sleeping bags, but along with the other volunteers, I wanted to show them how much Jesus loved them by taking an interest in them, listening to their stories and providing food for them. We discussed God's purpose for their lives, inspiring them to believe they have a future even if their past hadn't offered them much.

When they arrived at the Coffee Bar, the women were teamed up with the women volunteers on one side of the room and the men, with the men on the other side. That was a wise thing to do. Spending time with them was satisfying as I knew I was making a difference. I quickly developed a good rapport with them and looked forward to continuing my conversation each week. Working with my team was an effective way of sowing seeds into their lives. If we are uncomfortable reaching out on our own, working with a team in the community is something we can all do easily. Giving up our time really blessed us as we were able to make a difference to those special homeless people. It was challenging at times but very rewarding!

> *"And I have been a constant example of how you can help those in need by working hard. You should remember the words of the Lord Jesus: 'It is more blessed to give than to receive.'"*
> Acts 20:35

CHAPTER 15

"A Cup Of Tea, Dad?" "Oh, Yes Please!!!"

"Imagine who you want
your kids to become.
Be that."

THOSE WHO KNOW ME know that I love telling jokes; this is one of my favourites:

Three sisters, ages 92, 94, and 96, lived in a house together. One night, the 96-year-old ran her bath. She put one foot in the bath and paused. Yelling down the stairs, she asked, "Was I getting in the bath or out of the bath?" The 94-year-old yelled back, "I don't know, I'll come up and see." As she started going up the stairs, she paused and yelled, "Was I going up the stairs or down the stairs?" The 92-year-old sitting at the kitchen table listening to her sisters shook her head and yelled, "I sure hope I never get that forgetful knock on wood." She knocked on the table for good measure and then replied, "I'll come up and help both of you as soon as I see who's at the door." 😊

It is good to find things that make you laugh when life gets tough. My siblings and I had an amazing Dad. He was a faithful husband to our Mum, and he loved us all very much. He worked very hard for us to have a good education. He became a Christian in his 40s but only decided to get baptised when he was 70 years old. He was baptised on the same day as our daughter Deborah, who was ten then. He then spent the rest of his life serving people in his community alongside my mother. Sadly, he developed vascular dementia in his early 80s. His car, which was his pride and joy (he would clean the engine weekly), had to be taken away from him as he had become a danger on the road. He would leave his house several times daily to look for it and regularly threatened to call the police, as he thought it had been stolen.

It had been very challenging looking after him, and it was also very sad knowing that his world had suddenly changed forever. Experts say that for dementia patients, their past has become their present, the present is their future, and the future doesn't exist because they cannot store memory. One of my treasured memories of my Dad was when I had to bring him to my home to look after him for a few weeks. Knowing how much he loved tea and doughnuts, I took him to Krispy Kreme to treat him to a doughnut. I hadn't realised how confusing it would be for him to choose one from the counter as he looked at the options available. I tried to guide him and showed him some strawberry-flavoured ones, knowing how much he loved strawberries. He looked at me, smiled, and then looked up again at the gentleman waiting patiently to serve him. "Could I have a meat pie, please?" he asked. The man's expression was priceless! I smiled, chose a doughnut for him, and asked for a large cup of tea, too (one thing he never struggled to ask for). Then I told him I would take him to Greggs for a meat pie after that.

In the middle of the COVID-19 pandemic, we had to find a care home for him. Taking Dad to the care home and knowing that he would leave his home for good was traumatic. We weren't allowed to visit the care home before admitting him to see if it was appropriate, and we couldn't meet the staff either. We simply had to trust the reviews on Google, and we prayed that God would surround him with caring staff who would love him and give him the best attention, just like we would. We couldn't take him to his bedroom to settle him down or see where he would sleep. It was devastating leaving him at the door of the home with all his belongings in one suitcase, his Bible in his hand and some family photo frames for the staff to hang up in his room. We couldn't tell him that he had to go into care as he would have been very angry with us, but it was the right thing to do. A few months earlier, he had put his life at risk by switching on the old gas fire in his home and forgetting to light it. He had also managed to turn the gas stove on, triggering the gas detector. When the gas alarm went off, he ripped it out of the socket as he didn't know why it was making such a terrible noise! He also called me 60 times a day because he couldn't remember that he had even spoken to me. I eventually had to block his calls as I felt as if I was the one suffering mentally! I FaceTimed him three times a day to ensure he was alright and hadn't fallen. What was so heart-wrenchingly sad was that as soon as he was in the care home, they wouldn't allow him to have his phone anymore, as they were worried he might trip over the charging cable. Contact with my Dad went from 60 calls daily to one FaceTime call a week, only if they thought they had time available! If I called mid-week, they would let me speak to him again, but it was just a phone call, and the line was terrible, and he couldn't always hear me.

I wrote letters for the staff to read to him and sent him laminated Bible verses with his favourite photos above each verse. I knew that he wouldn't be the only one benefitting from reading them. He was eventually assigned a personal carer, and she very kindly arranged a WhatsApp video chat with the three of us once a week. Each time the carer called me, she would ask me to tell her some stories about him, and she created a book of memories to remind him of things about his family each day. She asked me what activities he used to enjoy doing. I told her that my Dad used to love reading his Bible daily, and I asked her if she could do that for him. I began to realise that God was also enabling this lovely lady to hear His Word. I sent her a daily devotional booklet (The Word For Today, written by Bob Gass), and she would read that to him daily. When she called me, she would share what she had read from the Bible with him. I remember once she "confessed" that she wasn't sure what to read to him, so she had "cheated and read everything that he had underlined in his Bible." 😊 Before ending our video call each week, I would pray for them both and would also pray for the staff, that God would protect them and give them the strength they needed in that challenging environment. They would say "Amen" in unison, which was so lovely. She also shared exciting news with me about her upcoming wedding. I prayed for her and her fiancé that the preparations would go smoothly, and I asked God to bless their marriage. She really loved that!

Again, out of an unbelievably painful time, God had brought something good out of it. Six months had passed before we were eventually allowed to see my Dad in person. We were given permission to take him out for a meat pie and a cup of tea, but only for a few hours. My sister would take him out once a week for lunch, but he soon became distressed when returning to the care home, and we were then told he couldn't go out anymore. Dad died shortly after his 85th birthday and was promoted to heaven. Once again, I thanked God for the seeds that had been sown in the carers' lives. I'm believing that someone else will water the seeds where I left off and that they will bear a harvest.

> *"As for what was sown on good soil, this is the one who hears the word and understands it. He indeed bears fruit and yields, in one case a hundredfold, in another sixty, and in another thirty."* Matthew 13:23

CHAPTER 16

Take The Plunge

"People may refuse our love or reject our message, but they are defenceless against our prayers."
Rick Warren

SOME OF YOU MAY still wonder how you could reach out to someone you have never talked to before and are perhaps amazed that I had the courage to speak to Helen. Believe it or not, I still feel afraid or uncomfortable speaking to people about Jesus, and it's mainly because I don't want to be rejected. However, I have learnt that I need to forget about how I feel. God wants to use us all to introduce people to Him. I am so grateful for what He has done for me, and I will share my faith no matter how difficult it may seem. If they reject you initially, pray for them and don't give up on them. God may give you another opportunity to speak to them later, or He may ask someone else to talk to them.

As I mentioned in the *Preface*, I want to be able to "help to bring" as many people with me into heaven as possible - this reminds me of a story which may be familiar to you:

Once upon a time, there was an old man who used to go to the ocean to do his writing. He had a habit of walking on the beach every morning before he began his work. Early one morning, he was walking along the shore after a big storm had passed and found the vast beach littered with starfish as far as the eye could see, stretching in both directions. Off in the distance, the old man noticed a small boy approaching. As the boy walked, he paused every so often and as he grew closer, the man could see that he was occasionally bending down to pick up an object and throw it into the sea. The boy came closer still and the man called out, "Good morning! May I ask what it is that you are doing?"

The young boy paused, looked up, and replied "Throwing starfish into the ocean. The tide has washed them up onto the beach and they can't return to the sea by themselves," the youth replied. "When the sun gets high, they will die, unless I throw them back into the water." The old man replied, "But there must be tens of thousands of starfish on this beach." "I'm afraid you won't really be able to make much of a difference."

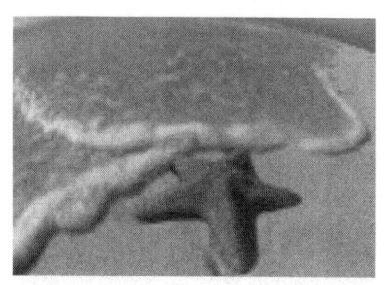

The boy bent down, picked up yet another starfish and threw it as far as he could into the ocean. Then he turned, smiled and said, "It made a difference to that one!" (Eiseley)

As you build up your confidence and share your story about what Jesus has done for you, you may find it easier to start with the people you already know well and are willing to listen. You can make "a difference to that one". We must remember that Jesus died for all of us, to forgive us and save us, and His desire is "that none will perish". As we share our story with others, we are doing His will and working with Him, and He will give us the words to say:

"For the Holy Spirit will teach you in that very hour what you ought to say." Luke 12:12

"The Lord is not slow in keeping his promise, as some understand slowness. Instead he is patient with you, not wanting anyone to perish, but everyone to come to repentance." 2 Peter 3:9

"But the Helper, the Holy Spirit, whom the Father will send in My name, He will

teach you all things, and bring to your remembrance all things that I said to you." John 14:26

"I tell you the truth, everyone who acknowledges me publicly here on earth, the Son of Man will also acknowledge in the presence of God's angels." Luke 12:8

CHAPTER 17

Christmas In The Sun

> "We cannot do great things on this Earth, only small things with great love."
> Mother Teresa

MY HUSBAND AND I, and two of our children, decided to travel to California for Christmas as I have several cousins who now live there. Christmas, for me, is even more special if it is spent with family. As two of our children have now married and left home, my parents have been promoted to heaven, and the rest of our family are scattered around the world, we seized the opportunity.

My cousin mentioned to me that she would be going to a Christmas lunch with her Bible study ladies, a final get-together before the end of the year, and asked me if my daughter and I would go with her. She wanted us to meet her friends. Before we made our way there, I asked God to give me an opportunity to encourage someone there. We drove for about an hour down the busy, sometimes nine-lane "freeway", being passed by some huge "gas guzzlers", the Dodge Rams being one of my favourites. The palm trees waved gently in the warm sea breeze. It must be wonderful living in this climate throughout the year. I couldn't believe that it was their winter and it was 20°C!! On arrival, we parked in the massive driveway and made our way up the stairs to the apartment.

We had arrived early, so I took the time to enjoy the stunning view overlooking the sea. Hanging in front of their dining room window was a water feeder, and now and again, a beautiful little hummingbird would come and drink from the sweet nectar-filled jar. Seeing how fast its little wings fluttered (80 times per second) was fascinating as I watched its long beak disappear into the glass feeder. Inside, the lounge was decorated with several miniature villages, similar to Lilliput Lane (miniature English and Welsh handmade models of real cottages and scenes). One village had a water feature, and another, a small train that journeyed around the model houses. Most of the houses were covered in snow, and some villages had churches with bells in their towers. I had never seen so many miniature villages in one home before. It must have taken weeks to put them all together!

Finally, the ladies arrived, and we were introduced. We struck up a conversation with a lady who had been born in Lyon, France, where my children were born. Who would have thought that I would end up speaking French in the middle of California!? Amazingly, she opened up very easily to me and shared her extremely difficult life journey. I realised this was the lady God wanted me to encourage, so I spent the rest of my time with her. She mentioned that she didn't want to come that day, but her husband encouraged her to go. She said she felt something or "Someone" had persuaded her to come and realised it was God. She shared a lot about her broken past but mentioned that she was on a journey, thinking about helping others who were as broken as she had been because she could understand what they were going through. I was able to tell her that it wasn't God's plan for her to have gone through those terrible things. However, He uses our painful circumstances and past so that we can help others avoid experiencing the same hardships. We can also help others stuck in those unfortunate situations and lead them back onto the straight and narrow path for His glory.

> *"Enter by the narrow gate; for wide is the gate and broad is the way that leads to destruction, and there are many who go in by it. Because narrow is the gate and difficult is the way which leads to life, and there are few who find it."* Matthew 7:13-14

I offered to pray for her, and she cried. I felt tears well up in my eyes, too, and sensed God's immense love for her. At the end of the meeting, when most of the ladies had said their goodbyes, the leader of the Bible study group came up to me. "You have no idea what an impact you have made on that lady today," she said. "I believe that God sent you to encourage her; it was a miracle that she even came to our lunch today!"

Overwhelmed by God's goodness, I left the apartment feeling so blessed that God had used me to make a difference in that precious lady's life. I was glad that I had taken the time to pray and ask God beforehand to give me an opportunity to encourage someone. Only God knows, but perhaps she may not have felt that "Someone" urging her to go if I hadn't prayed. I am blown away by the sense of strength, self-worth and satisfaction that I feel when I help to meet the needs of others. An unknown poet wrote, "It's loving and giving that makes life worth living."

CHAPTER 18

Who Would Have Thought?!

"You don't have to know all the answers to lead someone to Jesus. Sometimes just an invitation to church can change the direction of a life for eternity."
Gaynor van der Hagen

HAVE YOU EVER HEARD of Albert McMakin? Not many people have. He worked on the Graham farm and persuaded Billy Graham to hear evangelist Mordecai Ham preach when he visited Charlotte, North Carolina. According to his autobiography, Billy was almost 16 when he made a personal commitment to Christ during a series of revival meetings that Mordecai Ham led in 1934.

> *"Mr. Graham has preached the Gospel to more people in live audiences than anyone else in history—nearly 215 million people in more than 185 countries and territories—through*

various meetings, including Mission World and Global Mission. Hundreds of millions more have been reached through television, video, film, and webcasts." ("Billy Graham").

Here is a short story of Billy Graham's conversion:

Jesus Saves an Ordinary Farm Boy
The Story of Billy Graham's Conversion

75 years ago this month, Billy Graham committed his life to Jesus Christ. No one could have known then how God would use this ordinary farm boy to spread the Gospel throughout the world.

He thought they were fanatics.

One day in May 1934, 15-year-old Billy Graham came home from school and set out to pitch hay to the mules with one of the hired hands at his family's farm on the outskirts of Charlotte, North Carolina. The two heard singing from behind the barn, and the hired man wondered aloud what was happening. "I guess they're some fanatics that have talked Daddy into using the place," Billy replied.

Little did he know that he himself would be an answer to one of the prayers offered up that day during the prayer meeting being held in the pasture of his family's dairy farm. One of the men in attendance, a salesman named Vernon Patterson, prayed that God would raise up someone from Charlotte to preach the Gospel to the ends of the earth.

SPREADING GOD'S WORD BY TELLING YOUR STORY

Billy had been baptized and confirmed. He went to church each week, his family had Bible reading and prayer together, and he was vice president of the youth group at his church. But his real interests lay elsewhere. He hoped one day to play professional baseball.

That September, when an evangelist named Mordecai Ham came to Charlotte to preach at what would become an 11-week crusade, Billy wanted no part of it. After a few weeks, however, he became curious. Ham was known for pointing out sin in the communities where he preached, and he claimed to have affidavits stating that students at one of Charlotte's high schools were involved in immoral behavior at a house across the street from the school. Rumors then spread that students would protest at Ham's meetings.

These developments piqued Billy's interest. And then a friend named Albert McMakin said, "Why don't you come out and hear our fighting preacher?" Billy liked the idea of a fighter. The deal was clinched when McMakin offered to let Billy drive his dairy truck to the meetings.

After one service, Billy was hooked. He attended night after night, dutifully taking notes as Ham preached—and becoming increasingly convicted that he was a sinner who did not know Jesus Christ. He began to realize that neither his baptism and confirmation nor his church attendance would save him. "Our family Bible reading, praying, psalm-singing and church-going—all these had left me restless and resentful," writes Mr. Graham in his autobiography. "In a word, I was spiritually dead."

During each service, Ham invited people to come forward and receive Christ. On November 1, six days before his 16th birthday, Billy responded to that invitation. The choir sang four verses of "Just As I Am," followed by the hymn "Almost Persuaded, Now to Believe." On the final verse of that song, Billy went forward, feeling, he writes, "as if I had lead weights attached to my feet."

That night, he repented of his sins and prayed to receive Christ. And although he felt no great emotion, he knew he was a new person. His mother, Morrow Coffey Graham, recalled later that when she arrived home from the meeting that night, Billy threw his arms around her and said, "Mother, I'm a changed boy!"

In the months that followed, Billy grew in faith and began, sometimes shyly, to share his faith with others. Once, an evangelist named Jimmie Johnson stayed at the Graham home while in Charlotte, and Billy accompanied him to an evangelistic meeting at a jail. Johnson asked Billy to speak to the prisoners for a few minutes, introducing him as "a fellow who'll tell you what it's like to be converted." The prisoners looked uninterested as Billy spoke, leading him to think he would never be a preacher.

Billy Graham couldn't see the path on which God would eventually lead him. And during that *"pasture prayer meeting" the previous May, Vernon Patterson couldn't have known that a boy doing chores on the other side of the barn might be someone God would use in answer to his prayer. But looking back over the last 75 years, one can see how God called, prepared and led an ordinary young man to preach the Good News of Jesus Christ to nearly 215 million people in more than 185 countries.*

Are you praying for a loved one to be saved? Someone who shows no interest in Jesus Christ? Jesus taught that we are to pray and never give up (Luke 18:1). More than seven decades ago, God transformed a farm boy in Charlotte, North Carolina, in answer to prayer. You may see God answer your prayers in the same fashion. (https://decisionmagazine.com/jesus-saves-an-ordinary-farm-boy)

As Vernon Patterson had prayed that God would "raise up someone from Charlotte to preach the Gospel to the ends of the earth", and Albert McMakin had the courage to invite Billy to hear Mordecai Ham, God moved mightily and used Billy Graham's preaching to impact millions of people and *"According to his staff, more than 3.2 million people have responded to the invitation at Billy Graham Crusades to "accept Jesus Christ as their personal Savior." "Walk Worthy. What That Looks Like in the Life of a Believer."*

Billy said, "My one purpose in life is to help people find a personal relationship with God, which I believe, comes through knowing Christ."

Doesn't that impact you?! It's amazing to think about what God did through these people, how Billy's life was magnificently transformed, and what the result was after that!

Consider, too, that once a person is saved, their entire family could come to know Jesus too:-

> *"They replied, "Believe in the Lord Jesus and you will be saved, along with everyone in your household." And they shared the word of the Lord with him and with all who lived in his household. Even at that hour of the night, the jailer cared for them and washed their wounds. Then he and everyone in his household were immediately baptized. He brought them into his house and set a meal before them, and he and his entire household rejoiced because they all believed in God."* Acts 16:31-34

> *"I planted, Apollos watered, but God gave the increase. So then neither he who plants is anything, nor he who waters, but God who gives the increase."* 1 Corinthians 3:6-7

It's not about us; it's about God. Sometimes, we are called to sow, and sometimes, we are called to water the seeds that have already been sown. We can become discouraged when we don't see the results of our labour, but we can't see the bigger picture! God makes the seeds grow. When God prompts you to speak to someone, think of the possibilities and the positive impact that person could have on society just by you being obedient. That person could be the next Billy Graham and lead millions to Jesus!

CHAPTER 19

Don't Miss It!

"If you think you're too small to make a difference, you haven't spent a night with a mosquito."
African Proverb

DON'T YOU JUST LOVE that expression? It makes me smile. One person can make an incredible difference in someone's life by sharing God's love!

I believe these God-given opportunities will have made an impression on you, and I am so grateful for each of them. I am also convinced that Helen's story will significantly impact everyone who hears or reads about it. May we never miss another opportunity to tell people about His incredible love for them! God sent His Son Jesus to die on the cross for each one of us, to forgive us for our past and present sins, and to give us an abundant life ("until you overflow!").

"A thief has only one thing in mind—he wants to steal, slaughter, and destroy. But I have come to give you everything in abundance, more than you expect—life in its fullness until you overflow!" John 10:10

"For God so greatly loved and dearly prized the world that He [even] gave up His only begotten (unique) Son, so that whoever believes in (trusts in, clings to, relies on) Him shall not perish (come to destruction, be lost) but have eternal (everlasting) life." John 3:16

"And I will forgive their wickedness, and I will never again remember their sins." Hebrews 8:12

"Come now, let's settle this," says the Lord. "Though your sins are like scarlet, I will make them as white as snow. Though they are red like crimson, I will make them as white as wool." Isaiah 1:18

To conclude, I want to share one more story with you:

I was 23 years old when I realised I needed to be more proactive with regard to telling people about God and inviting them to church. I distinctly remember sitting in my apartment one morning and telling God, "Today is the day I'm going to speak to someone about You." I decided that I would find someone to chat with on the bus when I was on my way to work. When my bus arrived, I sat down and looked around. I felt the Holy Spirit prompting me to speak to a gentleman sitting opposite me. I tried to string a sentence together in my mind before starting a conversation. How was I to begin? My heart was pounding in my chest, and I was aware that I had been sitting there for some time. My stop was fast approaching, and I knew I would miss the opportunity if I didn't speak up soon. I just couldn't do it, but just at the moment when I had come to terms with my inability to speak up, the man started to speak to me. "I just want to let you know that God loves you," he said, "and we would love it if you came to our church on Sunday; here's the address." He leant forward and gave me an invitation to his church. I couldn't believe it! God had given me an opportunity to speak to a Christian to make my first attempt easy, and that gentleman had shown me just how simple it was! Thanking him, I took the invitation. The bus stopped, and I stepped off to continue my journey. I laughed when I told my husband at the end of the day what had happened.

Sharing my faith is most effective when built on a foundation of relationship and trust. Therefore, when I go to the shops, I try to go to the same till operator to get to know them. I chat about life in general and take an interest in how they are doing. They love to talk about themselves and their families, which makes them happy to know someone genuinely cares. If it's a lady, I will invite them out for a coffee when it feels like we have become friends. When the moment is right, for example, when my church is organising a special event for Christmas or Easter, I will invite them to come to church and pray that they will encounter God. If there is one thing to remember from reading this book, let it be this:

The only reason we should be reaching out to people is because we love God, and we love people. I have learnt that the antidote to fear is to love, as love drives out all fear. Our primary calling should be to walk into our world and be a blessing wherever we go.

Finally, it is not only about leading someone to make a decision to follow Christ; it is much more than that. It's about discipleship, too. One needs to be encouraged to get plugged into a Spirit-filled Bible-believing church where they can be discipled. Once they have given their lives to Jesus, it's as if they are beginning a new chapter in a book. Discipleship is an ongoing process, and one should never stop learning and growing in our walk with Jesus. Just as the disciples chose to follow Jesus, we should continually learn and grow stronger in our relationship with Him. It is impossible to do this by staying at home.

> *"And let us not neglect our meeting together, as some people do, but encourage one another, especially now that the day of his return is drawing near."* Hebrews 10:25

Discipleship training takes commitment, vision and an understanding of the Scriptures. In reading the words of Jesus, we see that discipleship is not optional for believers; it is the mission and purpose of the Church. We are to equip and train disciples, who in turn go out to equip and disciple others. When we have a joy-filled, love-filled heart, with the excitement of a better life and the promise of eternity with Christ, how can we help but want to share it with the world?

> *"Then Jesus came to them and said, 'All authority in heaven and on earth has been given to me. Therefore go and make disciples of all nations, baptizing them in the name of the Father and of the Son and of the Holy Spirit, and teaching them to obey everything I have commanded you. And surely I am with you always, to the very end of the age."* Matthew 28:18-20

> *"For God did not send his Son into the world to condemn the world, but to save the world through him."* John 3:17

We need to repent, be transformed and equipped.

I pray that as you have read about these amazing encounters, your eyes will now be open to "see" the opportunities that God will give you to tell someone in your world about Jesus.

> *"Don't stop! Keep on singing! Make his name famous!*
>
> *Tell everyone every day how wonderful he is.*
>
> *Give them the good news of our great Savior.*
>
> *Take the message of his glory and miracles to every nation.*

Tell them about all the amazing things he has done." Psalm 96:2-3

God has handpicked you to release life in your sphere of influence. He's given you a unique grace to reach out to your neighbours, friends, colleagues and family. You may be given an opportunity to speak with someone you know, or it may be someone you 'randomly' meet. Allow the Holy Spirit to lead you.

People are looking for Jesus; they just don't realise it yet. Start today and spend time praying for opportunities to make His name famous and for boldness to share every day the good news of Jesus with everyone.

CHAPTER 20

How Can I Pray For The Lost?

"To be a Christian without prayer is no more possible than to be alive without breathing."
Martin Luther

USING THE "HEART" ACRONYM for prayer:

H Pray for receptive **Hearts** - pray for your loved ones by name, that they will be receptive to the Gospel. Pray for the soil of their hearts to be prepared to receive Jesus.

E Pray for spiritual **Eyes** to be opened - bind what blinds their minds so they can see clearly and recognise Jesus. Pull down every high thing that exalts itself against the knowledge of Jesus.

A **Ask** "The Lord of the harvest" to send workers. Your prayers will not only position your loved one before Jesus, but also position them before other believers.

R Pray that they will **Repent** and believe, that they will not only become aware of their sin but also believe and receive what Jesus did on the cross and experience the hope that comes from giving their life to Him.

T Pray for **Transformed** lives. Anyone who is united with Christ is given a fresh start, a new creation. The old life is gone; a new life emerges.

CHAPTER 21

How Can I Accept Jesus as My Lord and Saviour?

"Christ died for you individually just as much as if you'd been the only man in the world."
C.S. Lewis

I want to let you know that Jesus loves you; He wants to have a relationship with you and to give you a life full of joy and purpose. Why do you need Him in your life?

1) You Have A Past

You can't go back, but He can. The Bible says,

"Jesus Christ is the same yesterday, today, and forever." Hebrews 13:8

He can walk into those places of sin and failure, wipe the slate clean and give you a new beginning.

2) You Need A Friend

Jesus knows the worst about you, yet He believes the best. Why? Because He sees you not as you are, but as you will be when He completes His work in you. What an amazing friend!

3) He Holds The Future

Who else are you going to trust? In His hands you are safe and secure - today, tomorrow and for eternity. His Word says,

> *"For I know the plans I have for you, says the Lord. They are plans for good and not for evil, to give you a future and a hope. In those days when you pray, I will listen. You will find me when you seek me, if you look for me in earnest."* Jeremiah 29:11-13

Perhaps you would love to begin a personal relationship with Jesus today. Pray this prayer right now where you are and invite Him to come into your life:

"Dear God, I am sorry for the things that I have done wrong in my life. I ask for Your forgiveness. Thank You for dying on the cross for me to set me free from my sins. Please come into my life and fill me with Your Holy Spirit and be with me forever. Thank You. Amen."

If you have just prayed that prayer, this is the most important decision you will have ever made in your life. Luke 15:10 says: *"In the same way, there is joy in the presence of God's angels when even one sinner repents."*

SPREADING GOD'S WORD BY TELLING YOUR STORY

Your next step is to find a church where you can be part of a community of Bible-believing Christians who can help you in your walk with Jesus. God Bless you!

EPILOGUE

HAVE YOU EVER LET fear hold you back from sharing your faith? In *Spreading God's Word By Telling Your Story,* the author reveals how fear of rejection led her to be silent about sharing her faith. However, after a heart-wrenching event, God transformed her perspective, shifting her focus from herself to the needs of others. This newfound compassion fuelled her courage to share her faith once again. The author's compelling stories reveal the many surprising ways and places the Holy Spirit prompted her to share her faith in Jesus. She also recounts how her obedience to the Holy Spirit's prompting opened the door for her to experience His presence in "*a new and unexpected way*". The author offers practical tips on sharing your faith and includes a prayer acronym on how to pray for the lost. She considers it an incredible privilege to help lead people to Jesus and encourage other believers, and she is convinced that, as Christians, we are all called to do the same.

Gaynor van der Hagen leads a Bible study group in her home, loves playing her violin, writing books and travelling. She and her family are actively involved in a vibrant and fast-growing church. She resides with her husband, Paul, in Surrey, UK. They have four beautiful children and a French Tabby called Leo.

REFERENCES

Works Cited

"Billy Graham." Billy Graham Evangelistic Association, https://billygraham.org.uk/billy-graham/.

Eiseley, Loren C. "The Star Thrower: Eiseley, Loren

"Survey: 60 Percent of Born-Again Christians Under 40 Say Jesus Isn't the Only Way to Salvation - RELEVANT." Relevant Magazine, 23 August 2021, https://relevantmagazine.com/faith/church/survey-60-percent-of-born-again-christians-under-40-say-jesus-isnt-the-only-way-to-salvation/.

"Walk Worthy." Therapon University,
https://www.theraponuniversity.org/ww/ww_21.html.

Printed in Poland
by Amazon Fulfillment
Poland Sp. z o.o., Wrocław